Educational Administration and the Social Sciences

Educational Administration and the Social Sciences

Edited by

George Baron
Reader in Educational Administration
University of London Institute of Education

and

William Taylor
Professor of Education
University of Bristol

THE ATHLONE PRESS *of the University of London*

1969

Published by
THE ATHLONE PRESS
UNIVERSITY OF LONDON
at 2 Gower Street London WC1
Distributed by Constable & Co Ltd
10 Orange Street London WC2

Canada
Oxford University Press
Toronto

U.S.A.
Oxford University Press Inc
New York

© University of London, 1969

485 11106 3

Printed in Great Britain by
WILLIAM CLOWES AND SONS, LIMITED
LONDON AND BECCLES

Preface

The increasing scale of educational provision and expenditure has given a new impetus to the study of ways in which educational institutions and systems are organised and administered. Hitherto such interest has mainly taken the form of historical studies of the development of the educational system, analyses of the legal structures within which schools and school systems are administered, and studies of the formal political processes, both local and national, associated with educational decision making. More recently, however, there has grown up a greater concern with the administrative problems involved in the determination of educational objectives and in the measurement of outcomes and there has also emerged a wide range of studies in educational planning. In the United States, furthermore, there have been extensions of the already massive volume of work in management, organisation and administrative theory to problems of school and college government.

In this country, despite the interest social scientists have taken in the processes of education and in education as a social institution, they have until very recently paid relatively little attention to the study of the form and functioning of its administrative structures. There are now clear signs of developments in this field and these essays seek to focus attention on some of the ways in which the thinking of social scientists may have relevance for both the study and the practice of educational administration.

It is hoped that this book may also serve two other purposes. One is to stimulate further work along the lines already being explored by the contributors, and to point the way for others, whether social philosophers, psychologists or political scientists, whose interests are of equal relevance for policy making and its execution in educational settings. The other is to show how the social scientist may contribute to the content of the many courses now being developed for heads and senior teachers, local authority officers and others concerned with educational administration.

The initial chapter by Baron seeks to provide an overview of educational administration as a new field of study and to suggest how issues faced by policy-makers and administrators can be related to the thinking and researches of social scientists. The other contributions then fall into two categories: the first concerned mainly with social science concepts, and the second with the application of the kind of thinking they make possible in the practice and teaching of administration.

In the first category Eggleston, Hoyle, Peston and Burnham are primarily concerned with present approaches and models that may be employed in discussing both educational administration in general and the administration of individual institutions. Eggleston concerns himself with the *setting* of administrative decisions and their examination through case studies, correlational studies and a systems approach; Hoyle presents one of the first analyses in this country of the contribution that organisation theory can make to educational administration; and Peston shows how the models of economics and the way in which the economist formulates problems can be of use in the study of administrative processes. Burnham deals specifically with role theory and shows its application to the analysis of school organisation and of head–staff relationships.

In the second group of contributions, Taylor, Owen, Austwick, Myers and Wheeler look at five key issues of practical significance for educational administration at the present time. Taylor relates the contribution that can be made by the social sciences to the preparation of teachers and others for administrative appointments, and describes some of the instructional techniques that he and others have developed for this purpose. Owen deals with changing concepts of curriculum development and control and their implications for the relationships between administrator and teacher; Austwick is concerned with the same relationships but in terms of the expansion of educational technology; and Myers provides an introduction to operational research as applied to education and gives specific illustrations of the work that is being currently undertaken in

vi

this field. Finally, Wheeler describes and analyses some of the consequences of growth in size in educational institutions, with particular reference to the technical college.

In the main, this book deals with the study of educational administration seen within the English context, but the influence of recent American, Canadian and Australian thinking is plainly evident. It therefore represents one of the first attempts to relate thinking about education policy and administration in English speaking countries through common patterns of thought and language. Nevertheless, the dominant note is that of English pragmatism; this is perhaps as it should be in a book emanating from a country in which the *practice* of administration has long been held in high esteem and in which its theory is only now receiving serious attention.

July 1968   G. B.

                                                                    W. T.

Contents

Analysis

Applications

Analysis

Chapter 1

The Study of Educational Administration in England

George Baron

Until very recently indeed, educational administration, as an *activity*, has been most frequently regarded, in common with other forms of administration, as a 'skill', an 'art', or a 'craft', proficiency in which was to be acquired in the solitude of the headmaster's study or, in the case of the young official, through working closely with an experienced practitioner. Such assessments were appropriate and fitting as long as change was gradual and the main tasks of leadership and administration were seen in terms of the perpetuation and strengthening of existing values and practices.

On the other hand, as a *field of study*, educational administration has paid little attention to contemporary practice. It has been looked upon as an aspect of the history of education, itself neglected by social historians, but fortunately cultivated in University Departments of Education. It has concerned itself with education as an aspect of social reform, with the evolution of central and local government agencies, with the provisions of acts of Parliament and the reports of commissions and committees, and with the campaigns of supporters of denominational schools for increased grants. Locally based research studies, few of which have been published, have been concerned with the tracing of variations in the general pattern of national policy, rather than with the processes by which decisions are reached in specific instances.

There are a number of reasons why quite new approaches to the preparation of educational administrators are now developing in this country and why the study of educational administration is nearing the 'take-off' point, at which it will join public administration and social administration as a distinctive and important field of study. Since the circumstances that attend the birth of any such field long continue

3

to condition its development these reasons are worthy of examination.

Foremost, of course, are those relating to the place of education in contemporary society and its government. Education is now accepted as a vital factor in social differentiation and social change; it is an important aspect of economic planning; and it is increasingly a matter of national and local political concern. Further, major administrative institutions are undergoing changes in structure that reflect the new functions they perform: the Department of Education and Science and the University Grants Committee are cases in point and even more substantial changes will no doubt follow in the structure of local government. There will thus be increasingly urgent need to review the relationships between teachers, administrators, elected representatives, parents and the general public. Policy-making, administration and teaching are tending to become ever more closely linked and this is exemplified in the Schools Council, one of the most interesting developments of the present time.

Equally pressing problems have followed the emergence of large scale institutions, both schools and colleges, with complexities of internal organisation and outside relationships of an order different from anything known before. The communications problems of comprehensive schools and technical colleges, the variety of links that they must establish with industry and other educational institutions, and their need to explain their purposes to the wider public all underline the scope of the challenges they have to face.

Before such demands learning by trial and error and with the help of seniors becomes more and more inadequate, and this is already admitted to be the case in industrial and commercial management. Hence the necessity increasingly emerges for practice to be studied, assessed and ultimately reduced to a form in which it can be taught to those outside the immediate situation. In all this, of course, recent thinking about education and the means by which it is provided, controlled and developed reflects the shift from the industrial society of the past century to the technological society of today. The essential characteristic of the latter is the application of study and research to all aspects of human activity, including those which, like manage-

4

ment and administration, have hitherto been dependent upon long experience and compliance with established custom and practice.

In addition to the demands made upon educational administrators by changes in the tasks they have to perform, there are others that arise from developments in the social sciences. Economists have become interested in education, not only as a factor upon which economic growth depends (Vaizey, 1962) but as an institution that can be evaluated in economic terms (Robinson and Vaizey, 1965). Political scientists are concerning themselves with political activity as it manifests itself in business concerns, voluntary associations and small groups (Mackenzie, 1967) and there is already some literature dealing with the part played by pressure groups in policy formation and execution (Cruickshank, 1963). Moving into the same area, but following their own specific interests and methods, there are the sociologists, with their concern for the structures and functioning of schools and colleges as social institutions. Finally, in some respects distinct from the three disciplines mentioned, but drawing heavily from them and from social psychology, theories of organisation devised to explain the working of industrial firms and other large-scale enterprises are suggesting new lines along which knowledge and research into the characteristic forms of educational institutions can be developed. There is, it is true, need for caution, since the structure and operation of any organisation derives from its purpose (Millett, 1966) but the value to educational administration of the approach pioneered in industry and the public services by organisation theorists cannot be disputed.

II

The assumptions and practices of the administration of education in England have grown from many different roots. They stem from the corporate traditions of the middle ages, the compromises resulting from the voluntary schools issue of the nineteenth century, the principles underlying the development of local government, and the demands of teacher associations. They also stem from the need to accommodate the aims of

5

humanitarian and social welfare movements within the sphere of education and from changing concepts of human interaction that created the factory, the firm, the club and the school itself. Viewed in the widest sense, as all that makes possible the educative process, the administration of education embraces the activities of Parliament at one end of the scale and the activities of any home with children or students at the other. Indeed, for its effective functioning an educational system must and does rely on parents performing both legally prescribed and generally understood functions. It is important to make this point, as otherwise there is a danger that 'administration' may be interpreted solely as the concern of officials of the Department of Education and Science and of officers of local education authorities. Indeed, the use of the term in England has been so limited that in popular usage it refers only to the latter category and is not applied to heads and others who are responsible for the organisation and running of the schools. Nevertheless, there is general recognition of the administrative nature of the headmaster's position, if still some unease at his being described as an *administrator*.

The ostensible separation of the teaching and the administrative functions was formalised in the middle of the last century, when the Public Schools Commissioners placed in the hands of the headmaster all matters relating to the internal organisation and discipline of his school and in the hands of the governors all matters relating to endowments and buildings. The division was elaborated by the Schools Inquiry Commission, which devised the tripartite structure of responsibility still reflected in the articles of school government at the present time. These state that the local education authority is responsible for the general educational character of the school, the governors for its conduct and curriculum, and the head for its internal organisation, management and discipline. The result is that the educational administrator in England has occupied a restricted role since many of the functions performed by him elsewhere as, for example, the drawing up of detailed syllabuses and codes governing the performance of teaching duties, have been carried out in this country by heads and senior members of school staffs. Examining, too, has been divorced from the administrative function and inspectors, at least at national level, have not had executive powers. Moreover, because education at the local level has not been a function of a separate structure but of an all-purpose authority, the education officer as such has shared with other local government officers responsibility for preparing estimates, for legal action and even for the staffing of his office and the clerking of his committees.

There is another complicating factor that must be borne in mind: this is the existence at each level in the controlling structure of an intricate system of lay participation in the making and ratifying of decisions: through Parliament, through local education authorities and divisional executives and governing bodies, and through a wide range of voluntary associations. Furthermore, over and above the agencies mentioned, there has developed an array of teachers' associations and associations of all forms of local authorities and providing bodies.

It is the consequent complexity of relationships and the interplay of pressure groups and interest groups at all levels that makes educational administration essentially political in nature. Save perhaps in the case of the simplest private school, what appear to be mainly educational or administrative activities are conditioned by political factors, and are resolved by some form of political process. Certainly this is true for the chief education officer presenting his plans for secondary school reorganisation, for the officer of the teachers' association preparing a salary claim, for the secretary of an examining board devising policy within the limits set by his board and his clients, and for the headmaster considering what line to take in respect of his parent-teacher association. It is important to realise that here the term political activity is not used in the sense of *party* political activity, which has significance only in respect of certain major issues. Even in these, as for example in the case of secondary school reorganisation, since local pressure groups of parents and teachers are involved, *party* politics is often far from being the only important element (Donnison and Chapman, 1965; Eggleston, 1966).

There is, then, every reason to look to the study of politics and of the political process as providing one of the bases on which the study of educational administration may be built, and this point of view has been reflected in the new approach to educational administration developed in higher degree courses at the University of London Institute of Education in the past four years.

III

But educational administration has just as much to gain from close affiliations with social philosophy, sociology, social psychology and economics. Even the most practical issues, such as those concerned with the siting and building of schools, the appointment of teachers and the subjects a child should study depend upon the interpretation at some point in the sequence of decision-making of basic concepts of equality, freedom and justice. Indeed, the educational system of any country is a major means by which the social values of its population can be either expressed or thwarted. Moreover, as Peters has pointed out, the justification of such values necessarily involves entering the realm of ethics and ethical theory (Peters, 1966).

There can be no doubt, too, that sociology in Britain has contributed very substantially to the common stock of general ideas upon which anyone concerned with decision-making in education must draw. There is, for example, the now well-established relationship between educational achievement and social class, that is already influencing educational planning and administrative action: and there is also a growing body of knowledge linking the linguistic skills of children with their home background. Sociological findings in these areas have very clear implications for the making of decisions in the political and administrative arenas. Where further development is urgently needed—and this can best be undertaken, as Burnham demonstrates, by sociologists working within a framework of administrative studies—is in respect of role theory applied to the relationships between, for example, heads and education officers, parents and teachers and administrators and inspectors.

Social psychology, like sociology, has concerned itself in the main with the pupil population, or with teachers in relation to that population. It is, from the point of view of educational administration, equally important that it should consider the functioning of committees of various types, the part played by teachers' associations in forming professional attitudes, differing patterns of staff and common-room relationships (Phillips, 1965), and various forms of reaction to inspection, in-service training, and teacher-education (Taylor, 1969). There is, perhaps, especial need for studies of the satisfactions and frustrations of the older teacher, and of the means by which administrative action can ensure that the later years of teaching can be more 'productive' and less frustrating. Until such studies can be carried out into school organisation seen from the point of view of teaching staff, the findings of sociologists and psychologists concerning the individual and social needs of children may tend to be resisted and resented.

The case for a substantial place for the economics and finance of education need not be argued, unless there is to be continued acceptance of the gap in thinking between those who are responsible for the allocation of resources and those who are concerned with their use. Failure to understand the economic significance of education has, it can be argued, resulted in under-spending at critical points in the past: it has equally resulted in unrealistic demands by teachers' associations and by reforming groups, and in unrealistic dissatisfaction with each reform as its financial implications have been grasped. The case for the study of economics by the middle-rank administrator and the teacher does not, therefore, rest upon its value as a 'tool' subject. It rests on the need, if there is to be a rational evaluation of educational change, for its cost to be assessed in terms of the sacrifice and effort required of the groups and individuals most closely concerned.

The difficulties in determining the content of any new and developing field of study such as educational administration must be regarded at the present time are considerable, and the chief, of course, is that it must seem to demand an impossible weight of borrowings from established disciplines. This, however, is to confuse a field of study with a curriculum. It is not to be suggested that a student should be versed in all the disciplines already mentioned: what is important is that his tutor or tutors should convey to him an awareness of the field

9

as a whole, and should be able to point out possibilities of development through co-operation with others. Such awareness will not, however, emerge simply from unstructured experience, and it is thus important that advances have already been made, as Taylor shows in Chapter 6, in the development of simulation exercises that seek to link the familiar day-to-day problems of the administrator with theoretical concepts drawn from social science disciplines. This, in large part, is the justification for this collection of essays.

IV

The approach to the study of educational administration through the basic social sciences is not, however, the whole of the story. Such studies illuminate the environment in which the administrator lives and sharpen his perception of issues and problems. But from the need for more specific understanding of how organisations work and how administrative functions are performed there has developed, over the past fifty years, a serious attempt to build up a body of theory concentrating attention upon the essential features of the structure of organisations and the way in which people behave in them. Stated in such broad terms, the history of this attempt is as old as human thought itself. In its present self-conscious form, however, it emerged as the scientific management movement of pre-First World War days, which sought to 'rationalise' human behaviour in the factory in order to maximise production. It was followed by a more liberal approach that stressed the place of 'human relations' and it has since branched out into studies of decision-making, general systems theory, information theory and various forms of organisation evaluation, and analysis.

The origins of the movement lay in the needs of large-scale business enterprises, and the major works in this field by, for example, Chester Barnard, Simon, Urwick and Argyris have been concerned with the industrial world. It has now reached out, however, to include political parties, hospitals and prisons (March, 1965).

In the United States the study of educational administration, as Hoyle shows, grew out of the need for the diffusion of practical knowledge about the administration of school systems among the many thousands of superintendents and principals who, compared with their English counterparts, were thrown very much on their own resources. It tended to be concerned, therefore, in its early beginnings, with the aspects of school finance, staffing, equipment, and school law that, in more centralised systems such as the English, were made known through regulations from the central department and through the activities of its inspectorate, through a common pattern of teacher training, and through the close interlinking of educational administration at all levels with the general administrative structure. During the past ten years, however, there has been a movement away from absorption in specifically administrative practices towards a concern with improving the quality of educational leadership. Concern, indeed, with the purely managerial aspects of the administrator's role has been supplemented by a realisation of the need to widen the understanding of superintendents and principals of the systems and organisations in which they work. The movement has also been signalised by an effort to get away from the narrow concept of school administration as an isolated phenomenon, and has sought to relate its content to concepts of administration derived from industry, commerce, the armed forces and social welfare agencies. This linked it with a body of thinking and writing, perhaps best typified in some of the work of Talcott Parsons, that aimed at generalising the organisational features of a wide range of institutions, and that led writers on educational administration to minimise the special content of their field. It led, too, to studies designed to help in the building of theory rather than to research into problems of immediate practical significance.

American approaches to educational administration, and especially those that stress the contribution that can be made from the social sciences, have greatly stimulated developments in Canada, and more recently still in Australia and New Zealand. In Canada progress was made possible by the establishment, with the aid of Kellogg Foundation funds, of the Division of Educational Administration at the University of Alberta, and the work done there has shaped the course of studies throughout Canada. Through personal contacts and latterly through the

University Council for Educational Administration, some basic concepts relating to the study of educational administration have been accepted in Australia and New Zealand, and at least made more widely known in this country. It was through the International Interchange programme of the U.C.E.A. that a group of British University teachers and administrators were able to join their counterparts from the U.S., Australia, New Zealand and Canada in the autumn of 1966. The first notion for the present book was a direct result of this stimulus, although the writer of this chapter must also acknowledge an earlier debt to the late Arthur Reeves and members of the Division of Educational Administration of the University of Alberta. Whilst the impact of these developments cannot be briefly assessed, it seems clear that a major result in Canada has been to give more substance to the roles of superintendent and principal (Reeves et al., 1962), by stressing their leadership responsibilities within what is often a highly bureaucratised provincial and local structure. To some extent this is also true in Australia where, with no intermediate policy-making body between state department and school it is of key importance that inspectors and heads should look beyond their immediate managerial roles (Walker, 1965).

In England much American writing on educational administration is of absorbing interest to the social scientist who is seeking avenues of approach to the study of school organisation and policy formation in this country. At its best it is charged with imaginative insights that throw new light on problems of leadership, structure and innovation. To the practitioner in England, however, writing of this kind can appear highly remote from his concerns, since the urgent needs at the moment are to translate into teachable form the managerial aspect of the headmaster's role, and to develop the mastery of administrative techniques that characterised the first stages in educational administration as a field of study in the United States. It is, therefore, of the first importance that there should be full and rapid development of short practical courses of the kind that are now being sponsored by the Department of Education and Science and that have already been pioneered by local education authorities and the College of Preceptors. But it is important also that awareness will develop of the wider issues that face those who are concerned with the shaping of the educational system and its institutions at a time when accepted custom has ceased to be a useful guide.

V

If the argument presented in this chapter has been adequately developed, it should now be possible to conceive of the study of educational administration in England as stretching from political science on one side of the spectrum of the social sciences to organisation theory and management studies on the other. Viewed in these broad terms, it becomes a study of substantial value, not only to those occupying administrative roles as education officers or heads of schools but also, because it is concerned with institutions with which all are in some degree familiar, to students specialising in one or other of the social sciences that contribute to it. It is clear, too, that as it develops understanding of the school as an organisation it can become of great significance in the preparation of teachers.

There are two major tasks that lie ahead, although beginnings have been made in respect of both. The first is that of making known and demonstrating the relevance of concepts and approaches that already exist within the social sciences and that have a bearing upon the study of educational policy and administration. Role theory from sociology, the concept of cost-benefit analysis from economics, pressure group theory from political science, group dynamics from psychology all have their special contribution to make. From these concepts and others related to them there may be built up an approach to the study of educational administration that gives it the theoretical bases of which it is so much in need.

The second task is, against the background just indicated, to construct, through investigation and research, a body of case studies from which systematic content can be developed. A number of such studies have already been made, or are in train. Some (Banks, 1955; Cotgrove, 1958) use historical materials and sociological modes of assessment to evaluate past policies and present trends. There are also more recent studies dealing with contemporary issues in policy-making that draw on new work in political science (Pescheck and Brand, 1966; Saran, 1968). The essential feature of these studies is that they examine the social and political structure of a single area and then analyse in detail the various agencies that operate in the creation of policy and the bringing about of change. Thus, what is of equal importance as the content of these studies is the methodology they suggest to the practising administrator, able to co-operate in or initiate studies in his own sphere of responsibility. The concept of the administrator, as well as the teacher, being equipped to contribute to the study of his special field must surely find early acceptance, with the spread of advanced studies and of research in education. All the more, therefore, is it essential to build up a framework of completed studies and a series of models to guide such efforts.

There is also a need for many more full-scale field studies of aspects of the administrative structure and its detailed operation, such as that into school management and government being carried out at the University of London Institute of Education (Howell, 1967; Baron and Howell, 1968). The importance of such studies rests, not only in their making available knowledge and experience that would otherwise remain hidden, but also in associating practising administrators with the work done in universities. For the latter they are vital if, in the words of Revans, it is to be possible to 'bridge the ancient gap between theory and practice that now runs round some of our universities like a stagnant moat, half-filled with corpses of ideas drowned in the rivers of change' (Revans, 1966).

There is, as yet, regrettably little going forward in the study of the organisational structure and administration of individual institutions. Descriptive matter has, it is true, been produced on the structure and functioning of comprehensive schools and more will undoubtedly follow from the major research project on comprehensive schools now being carried out by the National Foundation for Educational Research. There is also a competent narrative account (Firth, 1963) of how one authority set up its comprehensive school system, and the interpretative essays already referred to (Donnison and Chapman, 1965; Eggleston, 1966) dealing with the reorganisation of secondary education.

But there is nothing as yet, save one unpublished thesis, dealing with the internal structure and functioning of a local education authority (Brand, 1964), or with the post-war Ministry of Education,[1] and for this reason the sections dealing with education in Griffith's masterly *Central Departments and Local Authorities* (1966) are of particular importance. On the other hand, as Myers shows in a subsequent chapter, the *tasks* performed by local authorities in certain highly specific fields have attracted the attention of those concerned with operational research. Furthermore, beginnings are being made in the exploration of the role of the headmaster, and a first study of the politics of education in its English setting by a young Canadian has already broken new ground (Manzer, 1966). Then there are the very valuable studies contained in successive Year Books of Education, notably in a recent issue dealing with the economics and planning of education (*World Year Book of Education*, 1966).

VI

The purpose of this book and of the contributions that compose it is to centre attention upon the content and methodology of a developing field of study, rather than to discuss the kind of institutional setting it demands. But, as already pointed out, it is one that must be based on the expanding university studies in the social sciences. It is within the universities, indeed, that beginnings have been made in research in this field and they possess, in their Institutes and Departments of Education, on the controlling bodies of which local education authorities and teacher associations are represented, agencies designed to permit them to play a leading role. What is needed for them to do this most effectively is provision for separate departments or divisions of educational administration with staffs not so overburdened with teaching duties that they are unable to give time to field research and to building up the content of administrative studies. Developmental work, drawing upon the established social science disciplines and their research methods, is essential

[1] Although light is likely to be thrown on some aspects of the work of the Department of Education and Science by the enquiries of the Select Committee of the House of Commons now sitting.

if there is to emerge a substantial body of tested material, such as that already developed in Oxford and Bristol, for use in courses of a more specifically 'training' character. Perhaps one of the major mistakes in teacher training itself in the past was to base it upon the transmission of 'raw' experience and to fail to appreciate the need, met in schemes of preparation for other professions, for systematic study of the experience passed on.

Developments within the universities of the kind suggested would also fit them to make effective contributions to policy formation and to devise means by which it can be implemented. It is important, however, that the demands made by immediate needs should not divert attention from the studies in depth upon which the continuing satisfaction of such needs must depend.

Bibliography

Banks, Olive (1955) *Parity and Prestige in English Secondary Education*, London: Routledge and Kegan Paul.

Baron, George, and Howell, D. A. (1968) *School Management and Government*, Research Studies 6, Royal Commission on Local Government in England, London: H.M.S.O.

Brand, J. A. (1964) *The implementation of the 1944 Act in Leicester: a case study in administrative relationships* (unpublished Ph.D. thesis, London).

Cotgrove, Stephen (1958) *Technical Education and Social Change*, London: Allen and Unwin.

Cruickshank, Marjorie (1963) *Church and State in English Education*, London: Macmillan.

Donnison, D. V., and Chapman, Valerie (1965) *Social Policy and Administration* Chapter 12—Formulating a Policy for Secondary Education in Croydon, London: Allen and Unwin.

Eggleston, S. J. (1966) 'Going Comprehensive', London: *New Society*, 22 December.

Firth, G. C. (1963) *Comprehensive Schools in Coventry and Elsewhere*, City of Coventry Education Committee.

Griffith, J. A. G. (1966) *Central Departments and Local Authorities*, London: Allen and Unwin.

Howell, D. A. (1967) 'The Management of Primary Schools' in *Children and their Primary Schools*, Vol. 2. Central Advisory Council for Education (England), London, H.M.S.O.

Mackenzie, W. J. M., (1967) *Politics and Social Science*, London: Penguin Books.

Manzer, R. A. (1966) *Teachers and Politics*, A Study of the Role of the National Union of Teachers in making educational policy in England and Wales 1944 to 1964 (unpublished Ph.D. thesis, Harvard).

March, J. (1965) *Handbook of Organisations*, Chicago: Rand McNally.

Millett, John D. (1966) *Organisation for the Public Service*, New York: Van Nostrand.

Peschek, D. and Brand, J. (1966) *Policies and Politics in Secondary Education: Case Studies in West Ham and Reading*, Greater London Paper No. 11, London: London School of Economics.

Peters, R.S. (1966) *Ethics and Education*, London: Allen and Unwin.

Phillips, Margaret (1965) *Small Social Groups in England*, London: Methuen.

Reeves, A.W., Andrews, John H.M., Enns, Fred (1962) *The Canadian School Principal*, Canada: McClelland and Stuart.

Revans, R.W. (1966) *The Theory of Practice in Management*, London: McDonald.

Robinson, E.A.G. and Vaizey, J.E. (eds.) (1966) *The Economics of Education*, London: Macmillan.

Saran, R. (1968) 'Decision Making by a Local Education Authority', *Public Administration*, Spring.

Taylor, W. (1969) *Society and the Education of Teachers*, London: Faber and Faber.

Tropp, Asher (1957) *The School Teachers*, London: Heinemann.

Vaizey, John (1962) *The Economics of Education*, London: Faber and Faber.

Walker, W.G. (1965) *The Principal at Work: Case Studies in School Administration*, Australia: University of Queensland Press.

World Year Book of Education (1967) (eds. George Z.F. Bereday, Joseph A. Lauwerys), London: Evans Bros.

Chapter 2
The Social Context of Administration
S. John Eggleston

The examination of social contexts forms an important starting point for a substantial body of sociological analysis ranging from Durkheim's *Suicide* to Merton's *Social Theory and Social Structure*. Such an approach is particularly characteristic of the sociology of education and the exploration of the 'social class' contexts of educational behaviour has been an underlying theme of much of the empirical study which has dominated the field, yielding a number of well known studies (Floud, Halsey and Martin, 1956; Frazer, 1958; Bernstein and Young, 1967; etc.). A further group of studies (Coleman, 1961; Mays, 1965; Webb, 1962, etc.) has suggested that the roles of personnel in education are closely related to patterns and expectations of roles in the external social context.

The diffusion and imprecision of the goals of educational organisations render such organisations and their personnel particularly liable to contextual pressures[1]. The analysis of educational administration is unlikely to be adequate or even meaningful unless due attention is given to these; the often limited attention that such pressures receive in analyses of administrative systems generally is likely to be particularly disadvantageous in studies in this field. The purpose of this chapter is to consider approaches to the study of administration that offer the prospect of a more adequate consideration of contextual or extraorganisational factors and to suggest ways in which such approaches may be developed.

There have been a number of American studies that have explored the various aspects of social context in which the educational administrator works (Gross, 1958; James, 1967); though even here little progress has been made in the exploration of the

[1] Consideration of their 'external relations' formed a central part of an important preliminary study by Parsons (1958).

18

context of total administrative systems or sub-systems other than in texts which consider the issues in a generalised way such as *The Schools and American Society* (Selakovich, 1967). In Britain there has been little attempt to look at the context of educational administration. The less powerful position of local elected representatives on this side of the Atlantic and the way in which these representatives serve as a shield to protect the professional education service (both administrators and teachers) from much of the impact of external local pressures may partly account for this neglect. As Baron and Tropp (1961) have pointed out, the school system in Britain is largely insulated from direct social pressures. Detailed evidence in support of this view has recently been published (Baron and Howell, 1968).

The Evidence of Contextual Pressures

There is, however, no lack of evidence of contextual pressures on administrative behaviour in education. *Statistics of Education* (D.E.S. Annual, 1) regularly indicates important regional variations in administrative practices; *List 69* (D.E.S. Annual, 2) identifies a wide range of differences in local education authority practice with regard to secondary education, and *Education Statistics* (Institute of Municipal Treasurers and Accountants, Annual) confirms this picture with a wealth of detail for all education authorities in England and Wales. Perhaps the most striking demonstration, however, lies in *Circular 10/65* (D.E.S. 1965) which recognises clearly the way in which local contextual factors are able to superimpose a range of variations on national administrative policy for the comprehensive reorganisation of secondary schools. Six basic patterns of comprehensive schooling have been seen to be necessary in order to allow local education authorities to find a way of 'going comprehensive' compatible with local environmental conditions. The even wider range of local education authority proposals which have followed the recommendations of the Circular (documented in a recent progress report of the Comprehensive Schools Committee) have amply confirmed the expectation that a variety of possible patterns would be needed. Evidence of the range and consequences of contextual variations

19

within a local education authority is to be seen in the Robbins Committee discussion of the West Riding area of Yorkshire. It shows that it was possible to divide the authority into three areas for selective secondary school purposes, defined by high, medium or low intake into the grammar schools. As might be expected, the test requirements for entry into the grammar schools were highest where the selective entry was lowest. Yet a greater percentage of young people went to higher education from the areas of high and medium intake, suggesting that an important variable was not only the ability of students at eleven but also local policy on the provision of places in schools which prepare young people to enter higher education (*Committee on Higher Education*, 1963).

Evidence of the impact of contextual factors on the administration of the school is also abundant. The work of Mays (1962) and Jackson and Marsden (1962) illustrates the way in which the norms and values of the catchment areas condition the administration of the schools serving them. Administrative behaviour may also be modified by the conflict of values and norms between administrators and administered. This culture conflict is well expressed by Mays and also by Herriott and St. John (1966) who discuss the way in which the responses of head and assistant teachers in the catchment area are conditioned by their own values. A recent British study (Goodacre, 1968) reaches similar conclusions. Rogoff (1961) has held that there are distinct 'community factors' over and above the norms and values of the individual members of the area involving 'informal mechanisms such as normative climates or modal levels of social aspiration' which can powerfully affect the administration of education in an area.

Whilst all the studies mentioned so far provide important evidence of contextual factors that are significant in educational administration, none has been focused directly on administrative behaviour. Yet there are a number of interesting approaches to the study of administrative contexts that hold some promise of relieving the deficiency.

Case Studies

Perhaps the simplest approach lies in the case study technique which reviews a set of administrative decisions in the local context and examines any evidence of interrelationship between decision and context. Though such studies are still rare there are two recent examples which have looked at secondary reorganisation in two local education authority areas; Croydon and Northamptonshire, (Donnison and Chapman, 1963; Eggleston, 1966). Both used a pattern of interviews with involved personnel and studied official documentation, newspaper reports and other local commentaries to analyse the influence of established and specially created pressure groups such as parent-teacher associations, political and religious organisations, old pupils' associations and the like, and also the unstructured and largely informal pressures exercised by individuals using local media of communication. Both studies identify a very considerable degree of contextual pressure on the administrator's decision-making role.

Donnison and Chapman's study is of the preparation of plans for reorganisation of a group of long established secondary schools which, during the period under review, failed to reach fruition, due not only to the conflict between advocates of change and conservatism but also to the conflict within both groups of advocates. They identify a number of familiar features of the administrative situation:

the initial recognition of stresses calling for reappraisal of the system, the formulation of different—and sometimes conflicting—interpretations of this situation among groups with divergent frames of reference, the involvement of a widening circle of interests capable of exercising influence on the decisions to be made, and the concentration of pressures focussed upon the body responsible for those decisions.

The way in which the actions of the professional administrator are both precipitated by and subsequently modified by the interplay of contextual factors is clearly shown, as is the way in which such factors can override the 'rationality' of administrative behaviour. However, as Donnison and Chapman suggest in their conclusion, it is possible for the strength of the contextual factors to be intensified by the professional 'providers' of the service:

when important groups among those providing the service suffer, or expect to suffer, a serious loss of resources, powers or status, conflicts arise among them which will spread, if pressed sufficiently far, to a widening circle of outside interests capable of influencing the development of the service. The timing of decisions about this development then calls for sensitive judgment. For premature attempts to resolve such conflicts may commit those responsible for these decisions to standpoints which provoke unnecessarily intransigent opposition among those who must eventually play a part in the evolution of the service. Major participants in this evolution may then be compelled to resign, or evolution itself may be brought to a halt.

Eggleston's study is of plans to organise secondary education in a Northamptonshire new town where a conventional but only recently established pattern of secondary schools existed. Here the contextual pressures were polarised not so much into those for and against change but those for greater or lesser degrees of change. Partly because this distinction was not reflected by existing pressure groups and partly because of the relatively unstructured nature of the new town population the pressures were at first diffuse and fragmentary. But the study shows a remarkably rapid restructuring of the local community around new organisations—the militant left wing Association for Comprehensive Education standing for fundamental change and the *ad hoc* committee of teachers favouring only modest change. Though in the period under review the *ad hoc* committee emerged triumphant it is to be noted that, as in the Croydon study, there is no final resolution of the conflicting contextual pressures, merely a new and transitory equilibrium.

There is also useful case study material concerning school administration. Hargreaves (1967) in his study of 'Lumley' secondary school shows the way in which the context of peer groups, norms and values modifies administrative decisions to the school through relationships of compliance or conflict. A leading American case study is that of Clark (1960) who reviews the impact of client pressures for academic rather than technical careers in a Californian junior college. This led to fundamental changes in the organisation of the colleges including the development of new procedures for 'cooling-out' less able students, procedures which had been unnecessary in the earlier conditions where administrators had been in control of entry to careers.

Correlation Studies

Information that is more generally applicable can come from correlation studies where specific aspects of the administrative context are surveyed and correlated with administrative behaviour. A study of the administrative decisions concerning the provision of the extended secondary education in non-selective schools in eight Midland local education authorities (Eggleston, 1967) correlated the incidence of extended provision with a number of contextual features such as socio-economic status and occupational structure of the areas. The results indicated that decisions by local education authorities and schools to provide extended secondary education were significantly related to a cluster of socio-economic factors in their areas. In general it was clear that in all areas where there was strong and effective support for 'staying on', the local authority was generous in providing a wide range of opportunity for extended secondary education, notably through policies of comprehensive provision.

In a recent American study, Minar (1966) related variations in the style and content of the decision-making process of school systems (local education authorities) serving areas with different social structures, those of 'high status and low social conflict' and those with 'low status and high social conflict'. The high status, low conflict areas had administrations with fewer formal procedures, wider discretionary powers for the superintendent and policy discussions focused more on curricular then financial issues. Precisely opposite practices characterised the low status, high conflict areas.

Many of the well known correlation studies in education offer some indication of the impact of environment on administration. Amongst many examples are the works of Floud, Halsey and Martin (1956) showing the relationship between the social class context of the school and administrative decisions and of

Coleman (1961), suggesting a relationship between the youth culture context and administrative behaviour.

Correlational studies of this nature can offer a useful basis for the application of techniques that examine contextual variables in attempts to predict future data and probable consequences of decisions of educational administrators. One is operational research, a technique which allows the calculation of changes in the 'output' of an administrative operation resulting from specified changes in the 'inputs'. It is usually conducted through a series of mathematical equations and involves the addition of regression analyses and other 'multi-variate' techniques to correlational studies. The exploration and development of operational research in educational administration in England and Wales has been pioneered by the Local Government Operational Research Unit (Myers, 1966), and is the subject of a separate chapter in the present volume. Of especial interest here, however, is the Unit's first report on an educational problem, *Staying on at School* (Robinson, 1967). This is a study of the factors influencing decisions to remain at school after minimum school leaving age, planned in association with the present writer, which reaffirms the significance of contextual factors in determining both the demand for extended secondary education and the administrative response to such demand. Analysis of this nature has been further developed by Friend (1967).

Systems Analysis

Correlational studies can also lead the way to systems analysis of educational administrations in which the total set of relationships in the administrative system and its sub-systems is analysed as a whole. This involves consideration of both formal and informal and internal and external relationships. Bennett has suggested, in an article dealing with the correlation between educational change and economic development, that 'within the general framework of systems analysis the typical beginning is with correlational studies of the interrelation of variables without prestating 'cause' and 'effect' (1967). Perhaps the most useful exposition of the concepts underlying systems analysis and their application to educational and other organisations is

24

in the work of Mayntz (1966), which is usefully supplemented by the critical analysis of Mouzelis (1967). The review by Hoyle (1965) shows the utility of these concepts in the analysis of the contexts of administrative behaviour. Useful parallels with industrial organisations are illuminated by the work of Miller and Rice (1967).

Closely linked with the systems approach and with operational analysis is the construction of 'macro' and 'micro' models of administrative behaviour. The 'macro' approach is usefully reviewed in *Handbook of Statistical Needs for Educational Investment Planning* (O.E.C.D., 1966) and offers a valuable survey of the range of contextual inputs for which allowance must be made in the construction of 'macro' models. The possibilities of study of this kind are clearly to be seen in the work of Stone (1965) who sets out a long term model of the total education system of England and Wales which brings together the human inputs into the system, namely the flows of students through its various branches, and the economic inputs—the costs of teachers, buildings and equipment. A focal point of the analysis is the 'decision spectrum' occurring at the point of the minimum school leaving age. In a subsequent article, Stone (1966) contrasts and compares the structure of both types of input and uses it to examine problems of time lag and demographic flow using output as well as the more usual input coefficients for the latter problems. As Stone notes, at this stage the analysis of the education system has become but a part of the analysis of the demographic system at large and the analysis of economic inputs to the education system has become a part of the analysis of the productive system at large. Other notable examples of 'macro' studies are the works of Moser and Layard (1964) in the field of higher education, and of Alper, Armitage and Smith (1967) in local education systems. There are important links between these studies and the earlier analysis of Parsons (1958).

At the 'macro' level a number of organisational analyses of educational administration have been attempted. A useful review of this field is that of Brown and House (1967). Even though most of the organisational models indicate an awareness of the contextual variables of educational administration such variables are, however, only considered infrequently and often

25

incompletely. Thus Getzels (1958) in offering an awareness of extra-organisational factors through his idiographic and nomothetic dimensions, nonetheless delineates the field as 'interpersonal perceptions and superordinate–subordinate consensus; the nature of institutional and individual conflict; problems of effectiveness, efficiency and satisfaction and the nature of differing leadership-followership styles' (Getzels, 1958, p. 150). Similarly the many studies of 'organisational climate' of schools and colleges springing from the work of Halpin and Croft (1963) pay little regard to contextual variables. In the few studies where consideration is given to such variables as in those of Feldvebel (1964) and Gentry and Kenney (1965), who related organisational climate to local socio-economic variables, the relationship is examined at a correlational rather than a causal level.

Systems Approaches

An approach in which the extra-organisational variables may be seen more clearly may lie in the construction of models of specific acts of educational administration, using them to identify operational contextual forces. An attempt to establish such a model around a small specific administrative act is that of Mood (1967) who portrays the issues surrounding a decision to use films as an aid to teaching high school biology courses, and, in doing so demonstrates the role of such analysis in bringing to light unconscious and untested assumptions of the school administrators about the contextual variables.

Mood is using a preliminary systems approach—'the viewing of a situation in its entirety with all its ramifications, with all its interior interactions, with all its exterior connections and with full cognisance of its place in its context' (Mood, 1967, p. 19). Such an approach is useful at the present stage in our knowledge of the effects of contextual factors. It offers an attractive means of bringing together the relevant results of the approaches so far reviewed. It also allows a considerable body of other sociological analysis to be related to this area of study and opens up the prospect of conceptual and theoretical development.

By way of example, a systems approach model of the decision-

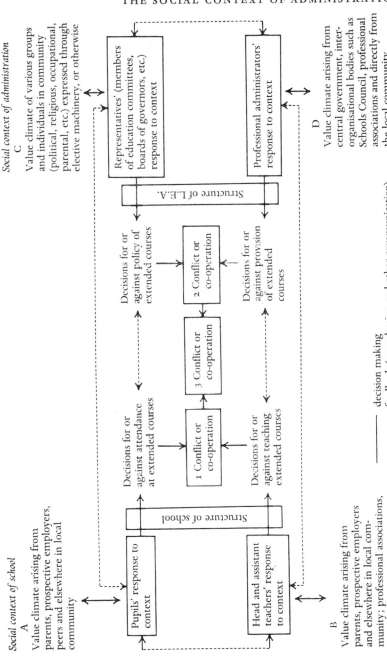

FIG. 1. Decision making procedure: provision of extended courses in a secondary school for the first time.

making procedure associated with the provision of extended courses in a secondary school for the first time is presented in Fig. 1. To make allowance for the interrelationship of contextual variables it includes four groups of personnel—pupils, teachers, representatives and professional administrators, and four corresponding groups of contextual variables:

A. Pupil Context } Social Context of
B. Teachers' Context } the School
C. Representatives' Context }
D. Professional Administrators' } Social Context of Local
   Context } Authority Administration

The groups of personnel and contextual factors are superimposed on a representation of the relevant structural order and lines of 'decision making' and communication are indicated. These are resolved, at any given moment of time, in conflict or co-operation, at the centre of the model (3). Two subsidiary areas of conflict or co-operation (1 and 2) are also indicated, in the school and in the administrative context respectively.

A simplified systems approach model such as this serves a number of useful purposes in the study of contextual factors. It enables known data on administrative contexts to be arranged meaningfully and in a way that highlights incomplete areas of information. It also shows the contribution of relevant areas of the literature of contextual factors to the understanding of causal relationships. Many of the contributions from the literature referred to in previous pages fall conveniently into place as aids to the understanding of the determination, strength and likely direction of the four categories of external variables shown in the diagram.

This 'ordering' of the data is seen as a key contribution of the systems approach. It is a contribution that offers the prospect of development in categorisation, conceptualisation and theory construction. Some examples of these prospects will be indicated by way of conclusion.

Categorisation

A useful set of categories can be established by the consideration of *conflict* in this area of administrative action:

(1) Conflict between choice made by pupil and choice made by teachers. The results may be 'no course', as in the studies by Mays (1962), or Webb (1962), or a compromise along the lines indicated by Hargreaves (1967), whereby the conflict is institutionalised. The choice of the teachers to mount an extended course is sustained by their ability to motivate a sufficient number of the more able pupils to alienate themselves from their peer and community background and join in this enterprise. Here, at surface level, the conflict is translated to one between two sections of pupils.

(2) Conflict between choices of representatives and choices of professional administrators. Here the result may again be 'no course', or a compromise solution whereby, for example, extended courses are only provided at colleges of further education or at a few selected schools involving transfer for the majority of pupils. The need to transfer between schools in order to obtain further education introduces an element of social selection, students with substantial home support for continued education being likely to transfer readily and those who rely on peer support for continued education being less likely to do so. (Eggleston, 1967 (i) and (ii)). In such circumstances the conflict may again, at a surface level, be seen as one between two sections of the student body. Or it may be translated into a conflict between the secondary and further educational establishments or between the two categories of secondary school.

(3) Conflict between the school and the professional administrative sectors. Again the result is likely to be an institutionalisation of conflict. This may take a number of forms in which existing or new organisations are brought in. For instance, the conflict may be formalised between, on the one hand, parent-teacher associations, teachers' organisations, associations for the advancement of state education and, on the other, denominational groups, political parties, and professional administrators. Or it may involve specially created organisations to preserve or to promote extended education such as local action groups, refurbished old pupils' associations or pupil organisations. An example of this was the 'school strike' at Gosford Hill School, Oxfordshire, in 1959, where an organisation of pupils formed to resist the arrangement of the LEA that extended courses

should be established at other secondary schools but not that one.[1]

There are many other possibilities for categorisation. Political, economic and religious representation may be categorised, as may be the various types of pupil, teacher or administrative behaviour in the face of contextual pressure. Such categorisation may lead the way to useful conceptualisation in this area.

Conceptualisation

A number of key sociological concepts may be applied to contextual analyses. The utility of the concept of *conflict* and associated concepts such as *conflict management* is clear from the discussion above. Similarly underlying system relationship mechanisms—*exchange, consensus* and *power* are evident. The last of these leads to the concept of *authority* (legitimate power). In the model used in this chapter there are four areas of authority—pupils, representatives, teachers and administrators—and the relative strength and nature of the way in which their power is legitimatised is of considerable importance in determining the resultant administrative behaviour. Part of the basis of this legitimation lies in the social context. Thus the authority of the representatives may be withdrawn entirely by shifts in the political, economic or religious context of the area (Gross, 1958; James, 1966). The authority of the pupils springs to a considerable extent from the context of the prevailing family, youth and employment structures. To a somewhat lesser extent the authority of teachers and administrators is also contextually legitimatised.

Consideration of power and its legitimisation is incomplete without consideration of the 'internal' power of the system which may, amongst other sources, spring from tradition, from law and from the personal characteristics of the individual. Internal power may be preserved or even reinforced by administrative action to bring about 'closed' education committee meetings and closed membership of governing bodies or, in the case of the school, by limited parental access and closed profes-

[1] Conflict categorisation is developed by Corwin in his examination of the goals of the school (Corwin, 1965).

sional ranks, all designed to meet the challenge from contextual forces. These are devices to ensure *boundary maintenance*.[1] Alternatively the administration may be characterised by its 'openness' and specialise in its accessibility and responsiveness to the wishes of pupils, parents, representatives and professionals —a response typified by Clark's 'Open Door' college (1960). A middle position ('swinging door') has been postulated by Litwak and Meyer (1966) who also consider the relationship between boundary maintenance and administrative style.

Theory Construction

Yet a further use of the systems approach model may be, as the review of categories and concepts has suggested, to act as a base for the formulation of theory. A useful example lies in the development of the theory of administrative change. Thus it is possible to hypothesise that changes in the scale, location and personnel of educational decision making may be related to shifts in the nature of social organisation—from a 'mechanical' society to an 'organic' society to use Durkheim's terms.[2] Such a formulation of changes in administrative decisions about extended secondary schooling is suggested in diagram form (Fig. 2). Though of necessity this is a 'general' hypothesis and need not apply fully to all secondary schools, it arises from the 'specific' model previously used, to which it is related (Fig. 1).

It is suggested here that the relevant contextual forces are changing in scale, content and location in accordance with changes in the social order and that this in turn is bringing about a shift in authority to pupils and students exercising personal choices. These changes, in turn, involve changes in the nature of the administrative decisions.

Further development of this and similar considerations opens the possibility of progress in establishing theories of administrative change with the advantage of the incorporation of adequate

[1] In the long run these devices are likely only to delay the response to contextual pressures and to intensify the ultimate change. As Goffman has noted, the more total the system the more extreme are the modes of adaptation (Goffman, 1958).

[2] The hypothesis that changes in the internal organisation of schools may be related to such shifts in social organisation has recently been elaborated by Bernstein (1967).

Contextual variables

Social Context of the School

Social Context of Local Authority Administration

A Pupil Context

B Teachers' Context

C Representatives' Context

D Professional Administrators' Context

Central decisions made by:	*Relevant structural order*	*Unit of decision*	*Nature of decision*	*Relevant local contextual forces exercised*
(1) Central government	Societal stratification	National	Extended courses in selective schools only. Personnel determined by 11+	All on number of selective school places. A and B indirectly through 11+ performance.
(2) Representatives and professional administrators	Localised stratification	Local education authority	Extended courses in some non-selective schools	C and D directly A and B indirectly
(3) Teachers	Intra-organisational stratification	School	Extended courses in school	B directly A, C and D indirectly
(4) Pupil/student	Individual differentiation	Pupil/student	Attendance at extended courses	A directly B, C and D indirectly

FIG. 2. Changes in decision making procedures; provision of extended courses in a secondary school for the first time.

attention to both the structural order and the local contextual factors. There are, of course, other areas of theoretical development of contextual studies which can arise from the systems approach. For example, consideration may be given to the differing perceptions of extraorganisational factors by the various personnel involved in decision-making. The objective of the chapter is served, however, by the demonstration that a systems approach and its extensions can meaningfully and usefully order the data, and that it can complement the understanding offered by the other approaches to contextual analyses of educational administration outlined in the first part of the paper.

Summary

The contextual analysis of administration is seen to be of particular relevance to educational administration with its characteristically imprecise and diffuse goals. The unstudied nature of much of the area is considered and the existing data and existing and prospective study approaches are reviewed. A systems approach is applied to a specific act of educational administration in order to develop a model to illustrate and clarify extraorganisational pressures and this in turn is used to sketch categorisations, conceptualisations and theoretical developments that take account of contextual factors. The justification for the model at this stage, however, is seen to be in its capacity to order the data meaningfully and usefully.

Bibliography

Alper, P., Armitage, P. and Smith, C. (1967) 'Educational Models, Manpower Planning and Control', *Operational Research Quarterly*, XVIII, 2.

Baron, G. and Howell, D. A. (1968) *School Management and Government, Research Studies No. 6: Royal Commission on Local Government in England*, London: H.M.S.O.

Baron, G. and Tropp, A. (1961) 'Teachers in England and America', in Halsey, A.H., Floud, J. and Anderson, C.A. (eds.) *Education, Economy and Society*, New York: The Free Press of Glencoe, 545-57.

Bennett, W.S. (1967) 'Educational Change and Economic Development', *Sociology of Education*, 101-14.

Bernstein, B. (1967) 'Open Schools, Open Society?', *New Society*, 14 September, 251-3.

Bernstein, B. and Young, D. (1967) 'Social Class Differences in Conceptions of the Use of Toys', *Sociology*, I, 2.

Brown, A.F. and House, J.H. (1967) 'The Organisational Component in Education', *Review of Educational Research*, XXXVII, 4.

Clark, B. (1960) *The Open Door College*, New York: McGraw-Hill.

Coleman, J.S. (1961) *The Adolescent Society*, New York: The Free Press of Glencoe.

Committee on Higher Education (1963) *Higher Education, Appendix I*, London: H.M.S.O., 72-3.

Corwin, R.G. (1965) *A Sociology of Education*, New York: Appleton-Century-Crofts.

D.E.S.—Department of Education and Science (Annual, 1) *Statistics of Education*, London: H.M.S.O.

D.E.S.—Department of Education and Science (Annual, 2) *List 69*, London: H.M.S.O.

D.E.S.—Department of Education and Science (1965) *Circular 10/65: The Organisation of Secondary Education*, London: H.M.S.O.

Donnison, D.V. *et al.* (1965) *Social Policy and Administration*, London: Allen and Unwin, 201–99.

Eggleston, S.J. (1966) 'Going Comprehensive', *New Society*, 22 December, 944–6.

Eggleston, S.J. (1967 (i)) 'Some Environmental Correlates of Extended Secondary Education in England', *Comparative Education*, iii, 85–99.

Eggleston, S.J. (1967 (ii)) *The Social Context of the School*, London: Routledge and Kegan Paul.

Feldvebel, A.M. (1964) 'Organisational Climate, Social Class and Educational Output', *Administrators' Notebook*, xiv, 1.

Floud, J., Halsey, A.H. and Martin, F.M. (1956) *Social Class and Educational Opportunity*, London: Heinemann.

Frazer, E. (1959) *Home Environment and the School*, London: University of London Press.

Friend, J.L. (1967) *Policy Research for Local Government*, London: Institute of Operational Research, mimeographed.

Gentry, H.W. and Kenney, J.B. (1965) 'A Comparison of the Organisational Climates of Negro and White Elementary Schools', *Journal of Psychology*, LX, 2.

Getzels, J.W. (1958) 'Administration as a Social Process', in Halpin, A.W. (ed.), *Administrative Theory in Education*, Chicago: Midwest Administration Center.

Goffman, E. (1958) *Asylums*, New York: Doubleday.

Goodacre, E.J. (1968) *Teachers and Their Pupils' Home Backgrounds*, National Foundation for Educational Research.

Gross, N. (1958) *Who Runs our Schools?*, New York: Wiley.

Halpin, A.W. and Croft, D.B. (1965) *The Organisational Climate of Schools*, Chicago: Midwest Administration Center.

Hargreaves, D.H. (1967) *Social Relations in a Secondary School*, London: Routledge and Kegan Paul.

Herriott, R.E. and St. John, N.H. (1966) *Social Class and the Urban School*, New York: Wiley.

Hoyle, E. (1965) 'Organisational Analysis in the Field of Education', *Educational Research*, vii, 2.

Institute of Municipal Treasurers and Accountants (Annual) *Educational Statistics*, London: The Institute.

Jackson, B. and Marsden, D. (1962) *Education and the Working Class*, London: Routledge and Kegan Paul.

James, H.T. (1967) 'Politics and Community Decision Making in Education', *Review of Educational Research*, xxxvii, 4.

Litwak, E. and Meyer, H.J. (1961) 'Administrative Styles and Community Linkages of Public Schools', in Reiss, A.J. (ed.), *Schools in a Changing Society*, New York: The Free Press of Glencoe.

Mayntz, R. (1966) 'The Study of Organisations', *Current Sociology*, XIII, 95–156.

Mays, J.B. (1965) *Education and the Urban Child*, Liverpool: Liverpool University Press.

Miller, E. J. and Rice, A. K. (1967) *Systems of Organisation*, London: Tavistock Publications.

Minar, D.W. (1966) *Educational Decision Making in Suburban Communities*, Evanston: Northwestern University.

Mood, A.M. (1967) 'On Some Basic Steps in the Application of Systems Analysis to Instruction', *Socio-Economic Planning Sciences*, i, 19–26.

Moser, C.A. and Layard, P.R.G. (1964) 'Planning the Scale of Higher Education in Britain; Some Statistical Problems', *Journal of the Royal Statistical Society*, Series A, cxxviii, 473–86.

Mouzelis, N.P. (1967) *Organisation and Bureaucracy*, London: Routledge and Kegan Paul.

Myers, C.L. (1966) *The Scope for Operational Research in Local Educational Administration*, Reading: Local Government Operational Research Unit.

O.E.C.D.—Organisation for Economic Co-operation and Development (1966) *Handbook of Statistical Needs for Educational Investment Planning*, Paris: The Organisation.

Parsons, T. (1958) 'Some Ingredients of a General Theory of Formal Organisation' in Halpin, A. W. (ed.) *Administrative Theory in Education*, Chicago: Midwest Administration Center.

Robinson, G.M. (1967) *Staying on at School*, Reading: Local Government Operational Research Unit.

Rogoff, N. (1961) 'Local Social Structure and Educational Selection', in Halsey, A.H., Floud, J. and Anderson, C.A. (eds.) *Education, Economy and Society*, New York: The Free Press of Glencoe.

Selakovich, D. (1967) *The School and American Society*, Waltham, Mass.: Blaisdell.

Stone, R. (1965) 'A Model of the Education System', *Minerva*, iii, 172–86.

Stone, R. (1966) 'Input/Output and Demographic Accounting: A Tool for Educational Planning', *Minerva*, iv, 365–80.

Webb, J. (1962) 'The Sociology of a School', *British Journal of Sociology*, XIII, 3.

Chapter 3

Organisation Theory and Educational Administration

Eric Hoyle

We have in Britain only recently begun to consider the behavioural aspects of educational administration, and our relatively late entry into this field makes it almost inevitable that our approach will be to some extent influenced by the 'new movement' in educational administration which has developed in the United States in the past fifteen years. It is the purpose of this paper to discuss the relevance of organisation theory to educational administration, with special reference to the theoretical orientations of this new movement.

The New Movement

Whereas in this country educational administration is generally thought of as an activity taking place *outside* schools and concerned with maintaining the educational system in good running order, the American usage equates educational administration with educational *leadership* at all levels of the system. And whereas educational administration in this country has been a largely unselfconscious activity generating studies only of a descriptive and historical kind, the American approach has been to view administration as a *process* about which it is possible to develop general principles for the guidance of practitioners. Theory construction in educational administration has passed through the same three stages as the construction of theories of industrial administration. In the early years of this century the leading American administrators such as Spaulding and Cubberly preached the gospel of efficiency in education (Callahan, 1962). But during the 1920's and 1930's, as the notion of 'rational' man was replaced by the notion of 'social' man, interpersonal relationships came to be regarded as the key to understanding educational administration, and this led to the

36

publication of a number of prescriptive guides to administrative behaviour and also of a number of more systematic approaches based upon theories of group dynamics. But the 1950's and 1970's have been dominated by the quest for more general theories of educational organisations embracing formal structure, inter-personal relationships, and individual motivation.

The following are some of the main characteristics of this new movement:

(a) A great emphasis on the need for careful theory construction as a basis of research and as a guide to practice (Griffiths, 1959; Halpin, 1967). Misconceptions about the nature of theory, e.g. that it is a personal affair, a dream, a philosophy, or a taxonomy (Coladarci and Getzels, 1955), are replaced by precise definitions, the most frequently quoted being that of Feigl: 'a set of assumptions from which can be derived by purely logic-mathematical procedures a larger set of empirical laws'. It is a characteristic of the new movement writers that they turn to the philosophy of science for guidance in their attempts at theory construction, and three particular themes emerge. The first is an emphasis on the need for operational definitions, although with indications of a reluctance to accept the full implications of operationalism, namely the view that a concept has no meaning apart from the operations used in measuring it. The second is a fondness for the use of models in research, although with indications of a reluctance to accept wholly the implications of isomorphism, namely, the requirement that the laws of one theory should have the same form as the laws of the theory which is taken as a model (Griffiths, 1963). The third is a devaluation of the role of classification in theory construction.

(b) An emphasis on the multidisciplinary nature of the study of educational administration. The social sciences in particular are held to be a fruitful source of concepts and theories (Downey and Enns, 1965; Tope, 1965).

(c) A rejection of the 'adjectival' approach to administration with a consequent emphasis on the need to construct general theories of administration which are applicable to educational contexts rather than to construct specific theories of educational administration.

37

(d) An approach which, with some exceptions (Graff and Street, 1957), seeks to make the study of educational administration value-free in the sense that moral judgments are avoided in the process of theory construction and values are treated as variables.

The serious consideration given to the process of theory construction by the new movement is a sound model for the development of a science of educational administration in this country. In particular we can learn to avoid the danger of 'naked empiricism' in our research, to dispense with the preparation of narrowly conceived 'cookery books' for the guidance of practitioners, and to adopt a multidisciplinary approach to problems. On the other hand, we must also recognise some of the present shortcomings of the new movement, and in particular those which have arisen from over-ambitious approaches to theory construction. Two such difficulties will be considered here. First, the tendency to overemphasise the importance of general theories of administration and to neglect the potential contribution of theories directly concerned with educational administration or even with the administration of schools. Second, a preoccupation with a socio-psychological approach to administration. But as will be made clear in the discussion, this is not regarded as an inappropriate approach but simply as an imbalance to be redressed.

The Quest for a General Theory of Administration

The efforts of the new movement writers to apply general theories of administration to educational situations have been hindered by such theories not having always succeeded in overcoming the limited perspectives out of which they have developed. Before looking at this problem it is worthwhile to raise the question of the relationship between 'administrative theory' and 'organisation theory'. An organisation embraces a formal structure and a formal process (i.e. administration) which involves such activities as decision-making, communicating, allocating roles and facilities, supervising and evaluating. It also embraces an informal structure and an informal process,

38

that is, the activities of the organisation's members which are not formally prescribed, and a culture—a pattern of values, norms, and their symbolisations. Thus administration is a sub-system of an organisation and not its entirety. *Organisation theory* is a generic term applied to all theories which have reference to some aspect of a complex organisation. *Administrative theory*, on the other hand, is a term applied to a theory which has reference to only the administrative dimension of a formal organisation and is subsumed under the general notion of organisation theory. However, another usage suggests that an 'organisation theory' is one which seeks to explain the structure and functions of an organisation as an entity by focusing upon one or more key dimensions (e.g. decision-making, the power-compliance relationship) regarded as crucial to such an explanation. Thus the terms 'organisation theory' and 'administrative theory' are synonymous so long as the latter, in focusing upon one or more aspects of the administrative process, seeks also to establish the relationship between these and the formal and informal structures, processes and culture of the organisation, and perhaps also the relationship of the organisation to its environment. The hiatus between the different connotations of 'organisation theory' and 'administrative theory' arises from the antecedents of current theories. In the main these are:

(a) 'classical' management theory pioneered by Taylor, Fayol, Gulick, Urwick and others, who applied engineering concepts to the problems of maximising efficiency in industrial organisations;

(b) the 'human relations' approach typified by the Hawthorne studies of Mayo and his associates, which had its origins in the classical management problems but which utilised socio-psychological insights in order to explain patterns of motivation and social interaction in the factory;

(c) the 'structuralist' approach which began with Max Weber's formulation of the ideal-type bureaucracy, based on sociological concepts and the comparative method, and which came to be concerned with the problems of all forms of organisation, for example, hospitals and schools, in a less action-oriented way than the previous two approaches.

These three perspectives on organisation have been converging at least since the publication of Barnard's classic *The Functions of the Executive* in 1938, and this convergence has in recent years led to the construction of a number of general theories of organisation. But although these theories occupy some common ground, they tend to have different orientations. Some are primarily administrative theories having relevance to the managerial problems of industrial organisations and utilising a neo-classical perspective. Others are more concerned with the integration of the individual and the organisation and display a neo-human relations concern with the problems of motivation, morale and satisfaction. Theories having a neo-structuralist orientation tend to be more concerned with the internal and environmental problems of organisations of all kinds, and to take a comparative approach.[1] But perhaps the most general approach to a theory of organisation has come through the application of the concepts of general systems theory, games theory, information theory and cybernetics.[2] General theories of administration or organisation are not invariably relevant to educational settings, and there are dangers in seeking to apply to such settings propositions derived from theories which are particularly oriented to industrial organisations or which are too general for the purpose. These dangers have not been completely avoided by the new movement writers.

The decision-making function of administration has often been treated as the central concept in theories of industrial administration (Taylor, 1965), and Griffiths (1959) has sought to derive from a decision theory a number of propositions which are held to be applicable to educational contexts, including schools. This is a legitimate exercise, for decision-making theory undoubtedly has much to contribute to the understanding of educational administration. But the ten propositions offered by Griffiths indicate the problems involved in seeking to utilise a general theory of decision-making, which may have been developed with industrial organisations particularly in mind, rather than to provide a more specific theory of educational

[1] For a brief historical treatment of the social science of organisations see Strother (1963), Gross (1964).
[2] For a general discussion of systems approaches see Carzo and Yanouzas (1967).

decision-making or even of decision-making in schools. The ultimate test of Griffiths' propositions must, of course, be empirical, but we can examine the cogency of the first three of these as they stand.

(a) *The structure of an organisation is determined by the nature of its decision-making process.* This proposition carries a certain conviction, but so does its converse that the functions of the organisation determine its structure and decision-making process. Thus the primary school, with its balance of socialising and instructional functions, is organised to facilitate a sustained relationship between teacher and pupil. This determines its 'flat' structure, its relatively informal decision-making process, and its balance between centralised decision-making and teacher autonomy. The secondary school, however, has the provision of specialised instruction as its major function. This generates a hierarchical structure with the *department*—whether academic or pastoral—mediating between the head and the teacher in the decision-making process. Thus in both cases the main functions for which the school is established determines its structure which, in turn, determines the nature of the decision-making process.

(b) *The individual's rank in an organisation is directly related to the degree of control he exerts over the decision-making process.* This proposition again carries conviction and appears to be almost self-evident, but one can again query its application to educational settings without qualification. It could be, for example, that the deputy head has less control over the crucial decisions of the school than the head of department, although his rank is nominally higher. The rank of the deputy head is probably more closely related to his latent power, the power which he assumes in the absence of the head, than his manifest day-to-day power. The proposition does not take into account informal power and professional power, which are more significant in schools perhaps than in factories. And outside the school, the proposition as it stands would not enable us to handle adequately the relationship between the headteacher and the divisional education officer or the LEA adviser. These problems can only be handled at the present time by a more specific theory of decision-making.

(c) *The effectiveness of the chief executive is inversely proportional to the number of decisions which he must personally make concerning the affairs of the organisation.* The truth of this intriguing proposition can be questioned on the basis of its congruency with another set of ideas advanced by Griffiths in a subsequent chapter of the same book. Here he approves of Barnard's distinction between three kinds of decision-making: *intermediary,* or that arising from authoritative communication from superiors, *appellate,* or that arising from cases referred for decision by subordinates, and *creative,* or that originating in the initiative of the executive concerned. But the implication of the proposition that the higher the number of creative decisions made by the executive the lower his effectiveness is contrary to the notion of the educational administrator as leader which pervades the new movement (Lipham, 1964), and also contrary to the research findings of Gross and Herriott (1965) and Halpin (1966). Moreover, it is incompatible with Griffiths' own later statement that: 'Ability and desire to make creative decisions is the merit of the top executive' (p. 102).

The importance of decision-making in educational administration is not in doubt, nor is its centrality to a theory of educational administration, but Griffiths' work illustrates the difficulties involved in seeking to apply general propositions to educational settings, and although the integration of a theory of educational administration with a general theory of administration is a desirable aim, perhaps it is more economical at the present time for the majority of students of educational administration to develop more limited theories.

The problem of over-generality can also be raised in connection with attempts to apply general systems theory to educational administration. The tendency to conceptualise organisations as systems has two sources which have become increasingly interrelated in recent years, the *empirical* and the *axiomatic* (Mackenzie, 1967). Empirical theories have their basis in the social sciences and are ultimately concerned with existential social relationships. The structural-functionalist school of sociologists, of which Talcott Parsons is the leading figure, has conceptualised social units as systems of interrelated parts collectively striving to maintain a condition of equilibrium. Further, organisational theorists since Barnard have regarded organisations as social systems seeking to maintain themselves through adapting to their environments.[1] Axiomatic theories, and particularly *general systems theory*, relate to a 'content-less' notion of system built upon a particular set of concepts, e.g. input, output, steady-state, feedback, equifinality, etc. Its original exponents were biologists, but it is now held that general systems theory can be used to conceptualise social, psychological, biological, ethological, physiological, mechanical and physical phenomena as systems, i.e. complexes of elements in inter-action.[2] In recent years there has been an interpenetration of the empirical and axiomatic approaches, and it is no longer easy to decide whether a particular set of propositions has empirical or axiomatic origins.

General systems theory has three potential uses in the social science field in general and in the field of administration in particular, but it is important to be clear on the use to which it is being put. First, it can integrate into one theoretical framework data from the behavioural sciences and thus lead towards a unified theory of human behaviour, (Grinker, 1967); and it can integrate this data further with data from the natural sciences to reveal patterns of organisation common to all phenomena. With this use in mind, general systems theory draws upon the theories and substantive findings of the separate sciences, but with the other two uses in mind the process is reversed and the separate sciences draw upon general systems theory. Thus the second use is to utilise general systems theory as a model in order to bring order to the data of the behavioural sciences and to reveal the crucial relationships in a concrete situation. Again there is no doubt about the value of general systems theory as a model of an organisation and its environment. It informs the

[1] For a brief discussion of the notion of *social system* see Parsons (1966, ch. 1). For a discussion of the application of systems theory to organisations see Schein (1965). The use of the systems approach in the social sciences is often criticised for its tendency to overemphasise integration, consensus and stability. This criticism cannot be taken up in this context, but see Gouldner (1959), Dahrendorf (1958) and, for a discussion of some fundamental themes, Meadows (1967).

[2] For brief accounts of the development of general systems theory see Mackenzie (1967), Griffiths (1963).

detailed models of the social scientist, suggests ways of ordering data, and has a general heuristic value (see Chapter 2 by Eggleston). The third use of general systems theory lies in its power to generate hypotheses which could not otherwise have been generated by a more limited theory. Griffiths has utilised general systems theory to generate propositions concerning organisational change (Griffiths, 1964). The following are examples:

> The major impetus for change in an organisation is from outside.
> Change in an organisation is more probable if the successor to the chief administrator is from outside the organisation, than if he is from inside the organisation.
> The number of innovations is inversely proportional to the tenure of the chief administrator.
> The more hierarchical the structure of an organisation, the less the possibility of change.

The heuristic value of these propositions, and the others which Griffiths offers, is clear (see Chapter 7 by Owen). The problem lies not in the force of the propositions but in their origin. Are they derived from general systems theory directly, or could they have been derived from a more specific theory and then *confirmed* by general systems theory? Propositions very like these have been generated and tested without recourse to general systems theory (e.g. Carlson, 1962). What, therefore, is the value of seeking hypotheses directly derived from general systems theory? Clearly to do this conforms to the requirements of parsimony, or the explanation of the maximum number of findings by the minimum number of propositions. But in our present state of knowledge about educational administration, this is perhaps rather premature, although there is a case for using general systems theory as a heuristic model or to reinforce the propositions of more limited theories. Grinker (1967) writes as follows:

Global theories are not usually operational. However, when they serve as umbrellas which encompass the subordinate theories that are close to empirical or experimental and experiential data, which interact but are not necessarily representative of the same frame of reference, they are extraordinarily useful.

This suggests that although we might find in general systems theory support of a *post factum* kind for more limited theories, we ought not, perhaps, to look to it as a source of hypotheses.[1] Merton's (1957) claim for the value of middle range theory is worth reiteration at this point:

I believe that our major task *today* is to develop special theories applicable to limited ranges of data...rather than to seek at once the 'integrated' conceptual structure adequate to derive all these and other theories. The sociological theorist *exclusively* committed to the exploration of high abstractions runs the risk that, as with modern *décor*, the furniture of his mind will be sparse, bare and uncomfortable. To say that both the general and special theories are needed is to be correct and banal: the problem is one of allocating our scant resources.[2]

A more limited approach to theory construction would enable us to handle the problems arising from the unique or limited characteristics of educational administration. There is, after all, little similarity between infant schools and factories, or even between infant schools and universities. One approach to these more limited problems might lie through typological studies. The more general sociological approach to organisation theory has been through the comparative use of typologies of organisations or organisational dimensions, (Udy, 1965), but only the more sociologically-oriented contributors to the new movement have utilised the typological approach (Carlson, 1964). Representatives of this movement have, in fact, been rather critical of the use of taxonomic methods. Halpin (1967) has pointed out that the use of taxonomies contains three snares: the assumption that verbal categories correspond to reality; the

---

[1] For a radical criticism of general systems theory, and especially the approach of James G. Miller, one of its chief protagonists, see Buck (1956).

[2] It ought to be stated here that at the present time there is a case for one or two people exploring the possibility of applying general theories to educational administration, but that limited resources will be most profitably used in generating and testing middle range theories. Although Griffiths' work has been used to illustrate the problems involved in applying general theories, it must be said that he has also been very much concerned with middle range theories of administration and with pioneering empirical research in the field. That he has diverted some of his talents to the development of general theory is to be welcomed. After making some criticisms of the social theory of Talcott Parsons, Andrew Hacker wrote that 'these criticisms should not be used as pebbles to derail the Twentieth Century Limited'. This is also true of the present writer's comments on Griffiths' work.

tendency to 'mix oranges and battleships'; and the assumption that a theory can be produced by the juxtaposition of two taxonomies. The terms *taxonomy* and *typology* both imply a scheme for classifying phenomena and they are usually used synonymously, but in order to meet Halpin's objection we can make a tentative distinction between them.[1] Thus we can use the term *taxonomy* for a Linnaean form of classification which is simply concerned with the identification of phenomena and hence is methodologically static. We can use the term *typology* for a Darwinian form of classification which is concerned with explanation and is hence methodologically dynamic. It would seem that Halpin's objection is to the exaggeration of the role of taxonomies, as the term is used here, in administrative theory. Perhaps the most famous taxonomy in the literature of administration is Urwick's classification of the functions of administration: POSDCORB (planning, organising, staffing, directing, co-ordinating, reporting, budgeting). In the field of educational administration taxonomies include Griffiths' 'tridimensional' concept of the Job, the Man, the Setting and the six types of school climate which Halpin derived by factorial techniques from the Organisational Climate Description Questionnaire. When the term *taxonomy* is used in this way, there is a justification for Halpin's point that a taxonomy is not a theory, although it may provide sensitising concepts for the process of theory construction. A typology has the power to generate hypotheses especially when organisations are being studied comparatively. Perhaps the best-known typology of organisations at the present time is Etzioni's nine-cell classification of power-compliance relationships (Etzioni, 1961). Blau and Scott (1963) classify organisations into four types: mutual benefit associations, business concerns, service organisations and commonwealth organisations, and then introduce a dynamic dimension by suggesting that the question *cui bono?*—who benefits?—generates a number of explanations regarding the different functions of the four types by focusing attention on the client-organisation relationship. Carlson (1964) has classified service organisations into four types according to how client control

[1] Although Burns (1967) denies a distinction between the terms *taxonomy* and *typology*, his discussion of this question (pp. 118–19) is highly fruitful.

over participation varies with organisational control over admission and he has utilised this typology in investigating administrative problems faced by schools. Although one would not wish to claim that current typologies of organisation have a high explanatory power, nevertheless they are a vital element in theory construction and do not warrant Halpin's strictures if, indeed, he would consider them to be what he terms taxonomies.[1]

Educational Administration as a Multidisciplinary Study

One of the most significant aspects of administrative science is its multidisciplinary character. In probably no other area of the social sciences has there been such a profitable co-ordination of different approaches. Economics, political science, anthropology, sociology, social psychology and individual psychology have all made substantial contributions, together with such infradisciplinary approaches as general systems theory, games theory, and information theory. Although theoretical formulations and research methodologies have been strongly influenced by a particular discipline, considerable cross-disciplinary borrowings have occurred. This has also been true of the study of educational administration, and it has been one of the strengths of the new movement that theoretical and empirical problems have been tackled without regard for the niceties of disciplinary boundaries. But having said this, one must not remain too complacent, for there are still certain dangers to be avoided.

One problem is that of eclecticism. Just as there are disadvantages in a narrow mono-disciplinary approach, so there is the danger of taking a broad view of administration which is not firmly underpinned by one of the social science disciplines. For this reason the term *multidisciplinary* is preferred to *interdisciplinary* since the latter could suggest an approach which, in its generality, falls between the interstices of the disciplines and adds nothing solid. A second problem is that of imbalance between the contributions of the different disciplines. It would

[1] For a critical discussion of the use of typologies in organisational studies see Mechanic (1963).

appear that the new movement has been dominated by a psycho-sociological approach which, in spite of the movement's concern to be truly multidisciplinary, has led to a concentration on certain aspects of educational administration rather than on others, and which has kept it very much within the human relations tradition of organisational studies. Corwin (1967) has made the following point:

Since the late 1950's several educational administrators oriented towards the social sciences have written on *human relations* in education (Griffiths, 1956; Campbell and Gregg, 1957; and Halpin and Croft, 1962). Like their colleagues studying human relations in industry, these men have been concerned with the problems of morale, the logic of decision-making, and styles of leadership and supervision of personnel. They have neglected the informal organizational structures, the essential organisational processes and especially the way in which the variety of structures and functions of organisations may affect learning processes.

This is a valid point. In theory construction and empirical work, the human relations approach has predominated over the structural approach. The exception to this has been the work emanating from the Midwest Administration Center, University of Chicago, which had had a more distinctly sociological component. What is perhaps the best-known model of educational administration—that of Getzels and Guba (1952, 1967)—originated from this source, and in taking *role* as its central explanatory concept mediates between the socio-structural (nomothetic) and psycho-structural (idiographic) dimensions of a social system (treated as isomorphic to administration). But it would appear that the hypotheses so far generated by this model have been mostly related to human relations problems in educational administration.[1]

Although the multidisciplinary character of the study of educational administration should always be recognised, there is perhaps a case at the present time for allowing this to emerge rather than aiming at it directly. Thus the danger of an invertebrate eclecticism would be avoided and the present predominance of the human relations approach—extremely valuable though it is—would be balanced by approaches having their

[1] See Sweitzer (1963) for an assessment of this model.

origins in a variety of social science disciplines. Mechanic (1963) has made the point well:

As an alternative to eclecticism there is value in a psychologist, an economist, a sociologist viewing organisations, each with his own viewpoint and approach. The relevant question is: To what extent does this viewpoint explain and predict the phenomenon in question? Thus, the psychologist may see to what extent he can account for organizational behaviour on the basis of personality variables; the sociologist may see to what extent he can push role analysis in achieving organizational understanding; and the economist might employ utility theory. It might be valuable to push these models beyond the levels of plausibility. Obviously, we must ultimately ask: What is the relative degree of variance explained by these varying approaches? And to what extent are these theories explaining different or the same proportions of variance? To the extent that these theories are complementary rather than overlapping, there would be need at some point to achieve synthesis for a more adequate theory of behaviour in question. But, to begin with, a tolerant eclecticism violates in large measure the principle of sound theory and research.

Other contributions to this volume view educational administration from the perspective of different social disciplines; the remainder of this paper will therefore be concerned to examine the distinctive contribution which can be made by a sociological perspective on organisations.

Educational Administration and the Sociology of Organisations

Sociological approaches to organisation theory largely stem from Weber's formulation of the concept of bureaucracy and subsequent modifications of this.[1] The main characteristics of the sociological approach are as follows:

(a) It is based upon a number of key concepts such as authority, power, conflict, consensus, which are also central to the study of all forms of social system and social interaction.

(b) It is concerned with both structural—formal and informal—and cultural characteristics of organisations and is concerned

[1] The key contributions to this tradition are contained in Merton et al. (1952) and Etzioni (1962).

to articulate these elements with the process of administration.

(c) It utilises historical and comparative approaches to organisational study.

(d) It has a special concern with the relationships between the organisation and its environment and with articulating organisation theories with more general social theories.

(e) It is concerned with all forms of organisation and not only the industrial.

Theory construction has developed at the following levels with respect to educational (and other) organisations:

(a) The application of a general theory of social systems (Parsons, 1966).

(b) The application of comparative typologies (Etzioni, 1961).

(c) The development of typologies of educational organisations (Carlson, 1964).

(d) The development of theories of educational organisation on the basis of certain key variables, e.g. role (Gross and Herriott, 1965), autonomy (Katz, 1964).

(e) The development of theories centred upon special problems faced by educational organisations (Selznick, 1951).

Although it must be admitted that at the present time sociological theories of educational organisation are rather few in number, we can nevertheless indicate several aspects of educational organisation which could be well handled through such an approach.

Organisational Goals

A special administrative problem arises for the educational organisation because the goal of 'education' is highly diffuse, and when translated into action gives rise to a number of difficulties. Firstly, certain educational goals are incompatible with others, e.g. socialisation and selection, critical thinking and conformity. Secondly, there is a constant need to affirm the importance of goals over organisational imperatives, and where this is not successful the organisation becomes an end in itself and the goals are subverted. Thirdly, goals tend to become scaled down to commitments which Corwin (1965) defines as the outcomes of a bargaining process between groups both inside and outside the school. There is a tendency for administrative theories to convert problems of goals into problems of decision-making, but in fact the diffuseness of the goals leads to conflicts within the school and its environment which are neither illegitimate or irrational, nor capable of being 'administered away'. Administrative theory tends to be orientated towards the achievement of consensus, integration and rationality, but the sociological approach to organisational theory is not so committed. It is true that some sociological theories employ a consensus model, but others are based upon the assumption that organisations are characterised more by conflict than by consensus, and that this is an inevitable state of affairs. The conflict model is not necessarily inherently better than the consensus model, but it does permit perspectives which elude many approaches through administrative theory.

Professionalism

A central problem of educational administration arises from the fact that educational organisations are staffed by professionals. But since these organisations are complex and require a central co-ordination of their activities, there always exists the potentiality of conflict between the bureaucratic mode of authority based upon status in the organisational hierarchy and the right to enforce rules, and the professional mode of authority which is based upon training and knowledge. Administrative theories of education often translate this problem into a question of leadership—which of course it is. But it is also a wider question which requires the conceptualisation of a link between conflicts internal to the organisation and the nature of professionalism, both in general and particularly in education. Corwin has conceptualised two role types for the teacher: the *employee* role which is characterised by rule-following, routinised and skill-based teaching and a subjection to a punishment-centred administration; and the *professional* role which is characterised by autonomous, adaptive and knowledge-based teaching and participation in a representative administration (Corwin, 1965).

These types are related to Gouldner's distinction between the *local* teacher whose loyalty is to his organisation, and the *cosmopolitan* teacher whose loyalty is to the profession (Gouldner, 1957-58). As Bidwell (1965) has pointed out, the school is characterised both by bureaucracy and by a structural looseness, and the need to balance bureaucratic authority by professional autonomy is a constant problem. It can be viewed in terms of leadership, interpersonal relationships, and organisational climate (Halpin, 1966). It can also be viewed in terms of broader changes in curriculum content and teaching methods. Bernstein (1967) has pointed out that new approaches to curriculum and method are likely to generate new forms of staff integration characterised by a form of co-operation which has much in common with Durkheim's concept of *organic solidarity*. Thus the internal problems of staff leadership have to be seen in relation to changes in professionalism in education.

Lower Participants

Theories of educational administration tend to be primarily concerned with relationships between the head of the organisation and his staff; the administration of the lower participants (students) is rarely considered. Yet there is clearly a need for the theoretical treatment of the impact of the students—especially in their peer-groups—upon the administration, and the impact of the administration upon the students. The importance of the peer-group as a locus of informal power in the school has been central to the sociological approach to schools of a number of American writers who have treated peer-groups as bearers of non-academic values, and who have seen the administrative response as protecting the 'vulnerable' academic values of the school against these pressures (Waller, 1932; Selznick, 1951; Coleman, 1961). Carlson (1964) has outlined some administrative responses to these pressures, including techniques of segregation, preferential treatment, and the substitution of custodial for educational goals. There have been fewer attempts to determine the nature of the impact of the administration upon the pupils. Revans (1965), working in this country, has demonstrated empirically a relationship between administrative relationships and pupils' involvement in schools, and Hargreaves (1967) has established a relationship between the formal structure of a secondary modern school and variations in the peer culture. The impact of peer-groups on administration and administration on peer-groups is not, of course, independent of the abilities of pupils and the values of their families (a point which will be considered below). Peer-group activity, however, is to some extent independent of these factors. There is evidence, for example, that schools which admit pupils from the same socio-cultural background have a differential socialising impact resulting in significant variations in the incidence of delinquency (Power *et al.*, 1967). In the absence of further evidence, we must assume that these variations are a function of the structure, administration or culture of the schools, or perhaps all three. These pieces of empirical work suggest the potential significance for the study of educational administration of theories which would articulate theories of organisation and theories of peer-group activity.

Organisational Boundary

Educational organisations, like others, have permeable boundaries through which external pressures impinge upon internal functions. Theories of educational administration have tended to be rather introspective and have focused upon internal problems. Where they have paid attention to external factors they have been largely concerned with the influence of the power environment of the organisation,[1] and in this connection have tended to draw upon sociological studies of community power structures. The sociological approach is also valuable in linking the internal organisation of the school with the cultural characteristics of the community from which it draws its pupils. The need for such articulation is clear from the work of Rose (1967). He hypothesises a theoretical relationship between staff values (emergent-traditionalist), organisational behaviour (formal-informal) and organisational products (high achievement, high aspiration) for a number of schools. An empirical relationship

[1] See Campbell (1957) for a discussion of situational factors in educational administration.

was established, but he also discovered that a greater proportion of the variance could be explained when the data were interpreted in terms of a typology of the communities from which the schools recruited their pupils. Other studies show that there are variations in the teacher's conception of his role, and also in how it is perceived by the administrator (Turner 1965), and according to the type of district in which the school is situated (Musgrove and Taylor, 1965).

Educational organisations have as part of their environment other educational organisations, and the commitments made by one might well affect the internal administrative policies of others. Clark (1960) has shown how the admissions policies of nearby institutions of higher education affected the internal policies of the San Jose Junior College, and it is clear that in this country, too, admission policies of universities and colleges partly determine the commitments made by schools. Clark (1962) has also discussed the importance of inter-organisational techniques which are bureaucratic, and patterns of political influence in situations of formal decentralisation. In this country also the agencies of educational research and curriculum development (e.g. the Schools Council, Nuffield Foundation, N.F.E.R.) are becoming significant components of the environment of the schools and likely to impinge with greater force upon their administrative policies.

A further point is that insofar as theories of educational administration have been concerned with environmental factors, they have tended to envisage the problem as one of the organisation defending its integrity against external influences. An interesting sociological theory which conceptualises the impact upon the administrative style of the school of its environment is that of Litwak and Meyer (1965). First they define seven administrative styles in terms of seven dimensions of organisation drawn from Weber's concept of bureaucracy. They then establish criteria for the evaluation of these administrative styles, given certain dimensions of school organisation and certain school tasks. Finally, assuming three types of linking mechanism between school administration and the community (open-door, closed-door and swinging-door), they discuss the possible relationships between administrative styles and these linking mechanisms.

These examples illustrate the point that the internal administration of an educational organisation can only be fully understood when articulated with a variety of contextual variables (see also Chapter 2 by Eggleston in support of this point).

Organisations in Society

The internal administrative processes of educational organisations can be fully understood not only in relation to their immediate environment, but also in relation to their broader social, political, economic and technological contexts. Burns (1967), after making the point that both 'natural systems' models and 'rational' models are introspective in their approach, states:

What is needed, not to replace this approach but to supplement it, is a conceptual scheme relating the organization to society in a way which will not relegate the latter to the position of 'environment' or of biological 'culture'. This involves the development of analytical categories that (a) identify organisations as functioning elements of society and (b) apply to the positive and negative consequences of the nature and operation of organizations.

This entails not only a conceptualisation of organisation-in-society in a given society and at a given time, but a conceptualisation which is historically and cross-culturally informed. Schools and other educational organisations have a history, and this is very much the history of the commitments which they make in response to societal pressures. Thus the student of educational organisations in this country could profitably draw upon the historical approaches of Banks (1955), Halsey (1961), Cotgrove (1958), Taylor (1963) and Blyth (1965) in their conceptualisation of current interactions between internal structure and process and the major social institutions.

The purpose of this section has been to indicate how introspective theories of educational administration might be rounded out through more distinctively sociological approaches to organisational theory. No single theory has been proposed. Instead, reference has been made to a range of empirical and theoretical studies which indicate some of the potentialities of this approach.

Conclusion

It has been the purpose of this paper to examine the approach to theory construction within the new movement in educational administration which has recently developed in the United States. It would appear that the quest for a general theory of administration which can be applied to educational organisations has not yet paid dividends, and this suggests that our efforts in this country should perhaps be less ambitious. It would appear also that the multi-disciplinary approach to educational admini-stration has not yet yielded balanced contributions from the separate behavioural sciences. For the time being in this country we should perhaps advance along mono-disciplinary paths in the hope that a multi-disciplinary approach will eventually emerge. In view of this some suggestions as to the distinctive contribution of the sociological approach to organisational theory are advanced. In all, although we have a great deal to learn from the new movement, we can perhaps learn from its present weaknesses as well as from its strengths.[1]

Bibliography

Banks, Olive (1955) *Parity and Prestige in English Secondary Education*, London: Routledge and Kegan Paul.

Barnard, Chester I. (1938) *The Functions of the Executive*, Cambridge, Mass.: Harvard University Press.

Bernstein, Basil (1967) 'Open school, Open society?' *New Society*, **10**, 259

Bidwell, C. (1965) 'The School as a Formal Organisation', in March, J.G. (ed.) *Handbook of Organisations*, New York: Rand McNally.

Blau, P.M. and Scott, W.R. (1963) *Formal Organizations*, London: Routledge and Kegan Paul.

Blyth, W.A.L. (1965) *English Primary Education*, vols. I and II, London: Routledge and Kegan Paul.

Buck, R.C. (1956) 'On the Logic of General Behaviour Systems Theory' in Feigl, Herbert and Scriven, Michael (eds.) *Minnesota Studies in the Philosophy of Science*, vol. I, Minneapolis: University of Minnesota Press.

Burns, Tom (1967) 'The Comparative Study of Organizations', in Vroom, Victor H. (ed.) *Methods of Organizational Research*, Pittsburgh: University of Pittsburgh Press.

[1] It should be noted, however, that certain key figures in the new movement are themselves fully aware of the present shortcomings of its approaches. See Culbert-son (1962).

Callahan, R. (1962) *Education and the Cult of Efficiency*, Chicago: University of Chicago Press.

Campbell, R.F. (1957) 'Situational Factors in Educational Administration', in Campbell, E.F. and Gregg, R.T. (eds.) *Administrative Behaviour in Education*, New York: Harper and Row.

Carlson, Richard O. (1962) *Executive Succession and Organizational Change*, Chicago: Midwest Administration Center, University of Chicago.

Carlson, Richard O. (1964) 'Environmental Constraints and Organizational Consequences: the Public School and its Clients', in Griffiths, Daniel E. (ed.) *Behavioural Science and Educational Administration*, 63rd Yearbook of the National Society for the Study of Education, Part II, Chicago: University of Chicago Press.

Carzo, R. and Yanouzas, J.N. (1967) *Formal Organization: a Systems Approach*, New York: Irwin, Dorsey.

Clark, Burton R. (1960) *The Open Door College*, New York: McGraw Hill.

Clark, Burton R. (1962) 'The Sociology of Educational Administration', in Culbertson, J. and Hencley, S. (eds.) *Preparing Administrators: New Perspectives*, Columbus, Ohio: University Council for Educational Administration.

Clark, Burton R. (1964) 'Interorganizational Patterns in Education', *Administrative Science Quarterly*, **10**, 2.

Coladarci, Arthur P. and Getzels, Jacob W. (1955) *The Use of Theory in Educational Administration*, Stanford: Stanford University Press.

Coleman, James S. (1961) *The Adolescent Society*, New York: The Free Press of Glencoe.

Corwin, Ronald G. (1965) *A Sociology of Education*, New York: Appleton-Century-Crofts.

Corwin, Ronald G. (1967) 'Education and the Sociology of Complex Organizations', in Hansen, Donald A. and Gerstl, Joel E. (eds.) *On Education: Sociological Perspectives*, New York: Wiley.

Cotgrove, Stephen (1958) *Technical Education and Social Change*, London: Allen and Unwin.

Culbertson, J. (1962) 'Trends and Issues in the Development of a Science of Administration', in Culbertson, J. and Hencley, S. (eds.) *Preparing Educational Administrators: New Perspectives*, Columbus, Ohio: University Council for Educational Administration.

Dahrendorf, R. (1958) 'Out of Utopia', *American Journal of Sociology*, **64**.

Downey, L.W. and Enns, F. (1963) *The Social Sciences and Educational Administration*, Calgary: University of Alberta Press.

Etzioni, Amitai (1962) *Complex Organizations: a Sociological Reader*, New York: Holt, Rinehart, Winston.

Etzioni, Amitai (1961) *A Comparative Analysis of Complex Organizations*, New York: The Free Press of Glencoe,

Getzels, J.W. (1952) 'A Psycho-sociological Framework for the Study of Educational Administration', *Harvard Educational Review*, **22**.

Getzels, J.W. and Guba, Egon, G. (1957) 'Social Behaviour and the Administrative Process, *School Review*, **55**.

Gouldner, Alvin W. (1957–58) 'Cosmopolitans and Locals: Towards an Analysis of Latent Social Roles', *Administrative Science Quarterly*, **2**.

Gouldner, Alvin W. (1959) 'Organizational Analysis', in Merton, R. *et al.* (eds.) *Sociology Today*, New York: Basic Books.

Graff, Orin B. and Street, Calvin M. (1957) 'Developing a Value Framework for Educational Administration', in Campbell, R.F. and Gregg, R.T. (eds.) *Administrative Behaviour in Education*, New York: Harper and Row.

Griffiths, Daniel E. (1959) *Administrative Theory*, New York: Appleton-Century-Crofts.

Griffiths, Daniel E. (1963) 'The Use of Models in Research', in Culbertson, J.A. and Hencley, S. (eds.) *Educational Research: New Perspectives*, Danville, Ill.: Interstate.

Griffiths, Daniel E. (1964) 'Administrative Theory and Change in Organizations', in Miles, Matthew B. (ed.) *Innovation in Education*, New York: Teachers College, Columbia University.

Grinker, Roy (1967) *Toward a Unified Theory of Human Behaviour*, New York: Basic Books.

Gross, Bertram M. (1964) 'The Scientific Approach to Administration', in Griffiths, Daniel E. (ed.) *Behavioural Science and Educational Administration*, 63rd Yearbook of the National Society for the Study of Education, Part II, Chicago: University of Chicago Press.

Gross, Neal and Herriott, Robert E. (1965) *Staff Leadership in Public Schools: a Sociological Enquiry*, New York: Wiley.

Halpin, Andrew W. (1966) *Theory and Research in Administration*, New York: Macmillan.

Halpin, Andrew W. (1967) *Administrative Theory in Education*, New York: Macmillan.

Halsey, A.H. (1961) 'The Changing Social Functions of Universities', in Halsey, A.H. Floud, J. and Anderson, A.C. (eds.) *Education Economy and Society*, New York: The Free Press of Glencoe.

Hargreaves, David H. (1967) *Social Relations in a Secondary School*, London: Routledge and Kegan Paul.

Katz, Fred E. (1964). 'The School as a Complex Organization', *Harvard Educational Review*, **34**.

Lipham, James M. (1964) 'Leadership and Administration', in Griffiths, Daniel E. (ed.) *Behavioural Science and Educational Administration*, 63rd Yearbook of the National Society for the Study of Education, Part II, Chicago: University of Chicago Press.

Litwak, E. and Meyer, H.J. (1965) 'Administrative Styles and Community Linkages', in Reiss, A.J. (ed.) *Schools in a Changing Society*, New York: The Free Press of Glencoe.

Mackenzie, W.J.M. (1967) *Politics and Social Science*, London: Penguin Books.

Meadows, Paul (1967) 'Towards a Taxonomy of Organization Theory', in Gross, L. (ed.) *Sociological Theory: Images and Paradigms*, New York: Harper and Row.

Mechanic, David (1963) 'Some Considerations in the Methodology of

Organizational Studies', in Leavitt, H.J. (ed.) *The Social Science of Organizations*, New York: Prentice Hall.

Merton, Robert K. (1957) *Social Theory and Social Structure*, Revised edition, New York: The Free Press of Glencoe.

Merton, R.K. *et al.* (1952) *Reader in Bureaucracy*, New York: Free Press.

Musgrove, F. and Taylor, P.H. (1965) 'Teachers' and Parents' Conception of the Teacher's Role', *British Journal of Educational Psychology*, **35**.

Parsons, Talcott (1958) 'Some Ingredients of a General Theory of Formal Organization', in Halpin, A.W. (ed.) *Administrative Theory in Education*, Chicago: Midwest Administration Center.

Parsons, Talcott (1966) *Societies: Evolutionary and Comparative Perspectives*, New York: Prentice Hall.

Power, M.J. *et al.* (1967) 'Delinquent Schools?', *New Society*, **10**, 264.

Revans, R.W. (1965) 'Involvement in School', *New Society*, **6**, 152.

Rose, Gale (1967) 'Organizational Behaviour and its Concomitants in Schools', *Administrator's Notebook*, **15** (7).

Schein, Edgar H. (1965) *Organizational Psychology*, New York: Prentice Hall.

Selznick, Philip (1951) 'Institutional Vulnerability in Mass Society', *American Journal of Sociology*, **56**.

Strother, George B. (1963) 'Problems in the Development of a Social Science of Organizations', in Leavitt, H.J. (ed.) *The Social Science of Organizations*, New York: Prentice Hall.

Sweitzer, R.E. (1963) 'An Assessment of two Theoretical Frameworks' in Culbertson, J. and Hencley, S. (eds.) *Educational Research: New Perspectives*, Danville, Ill.: Interstate.

Taylor, Donald W. (1965) 'Decision Making and Problem Solving', in March J.G. (ed.) *Handbook of Organizations*, New York: Rand McNally.

Taylor, William (1963) *The Secondary Modern School*, London: Faber and Faber.

Tope, D.E. (1965) *The Social Sciences View Administration*, New York: Prentice Hall.

Turner, R.L. (1965) 'Characteristics of beginning teachers; their differential linkage with school-system types', *School Review*, **73**, 1.

Udy, Stanley H. (1965) 'The Comparative Analysis of Organizations', in J.G. March (ed.) *Handbook of Organizations*, New York: Rand McNally.

Waller, Willard (1932) *The Sociology of Teaching*, New York: Wiley.

Chapter 4

Economics and Administration of Education

Maurice Peston

The idea that there is or ought to be a connection between economics and the administration of education springs from two different sources. There is first of all the study of the economics of education which, while its origins can be traced to the distant past, even as far as Adam Smith, has really only come to fruition and to public notice in the past decade. Secondly, there is the growing concern with the general micro-efficiency of government activity, starting from the *Sixth Report of The Estimates Committee* (H/C 1957/58) and the Plowden report on *The Control of Public Expenditure* (Cmnd. 1432, 1961). There is then a general concern with efficient operations in the public sector and the use of improved methods of costing operations, of programme budgeting (within the Ministry of Defence), of forward projections of possible requirements and needs based on well-defined explicit criteria, and of cost benefit analysis. At the same time, there is the application, actual or potential, of these approaches to education in particular.

In this essay I shall take the economics of education as my point of departure and describe the theoretical and empirical work that has been done in this field, in order to determine its connection with educational administration. It will then be possible to see what help economics and economists can be to education at both the national and local levels. Needless to say only the qualifications of the author and the advantages of the division of labour lie behind the emphasis on economics, and it is certainly not my purpose to argue that the only relevant discipline is economics and that the only important problems of educational administration are economic ones. Nonetheless, I would argue that too little attention has been paid to economic matters in the past, a defect which the Department of Education and Science is showing some signs of remedying. More strongly,

I would assert that educational administration has for far too long lacked a firm foundation of social science, and has proceded on a basis of hypotheses tested at best by common experience rather than by serious research.

It has also suffered excessively, as have all other parts of public activity connected with social welfare, from a serious confusion of the normative and the positive. Far too often value judgments have obtruded into places correctly reserved for the purely empirical, administrators and others mixing up what ought to be and what they desire, with what is and what can be achieved. The straightforward formulation of a problem, its analysis, and the bringing to bear of relevant evidence, all as careful preparation for the application of criteria of value are not the commonplaces of decision makers at any level of administration. Plunging in the dark, reacting to crisis, and making the best of over-commitment, are much more favoured activities.

The notion that the economic productivity of the labour force can be influenced by education is not at all new. Although it has been a useful simplification of theoretical economics to treat labour as a homogeneous factor of production, economists have long been aware that for certain purposes emphasis must be placed on variations with respect to skill, location, intelligence, and above all education and training. In considering the contribution of each of these characteristics to economic performance a number of points must be emphasised:

(i) The analysis of economic performance is multi-variate. Education and training are only two out of many variables which affect economic performance.

(ii) The variables contributing to economic performance may not be separable. This means that the contribution of any one of them may be affected by the level of the others.

(iii) The relevant dependent variable (or set of dependent variables) is likely to be economic performance over time rather than at a point of time. It follows that it is possible for more education to raise economic performance over some relevant time period although at some point of time it may lower it.

Although these points are commonplace they are frequently not understood, especially by people, including administrators, who are interested in education but do not have a suitable training in the social sciences. Even among social scientists those not used to constructing models and analysing them also seem to be confused on these issues. To take some simple examples; (a) there is no contradiction between the propositions 'economic performance increases with intelligence' and 'economic performance increases with education'. They are not competing hypotheses, but complementary parts of the same hypothesis; (b) the proposition, 'the contribution of education to economic performance depends on the level of intelligence' does not imply that the education makes no contribution to economic performance nor that any increase in education, other things being equal, cannot raise economic performance; and (c) education may raise economic performance even though people are taken out of the labour force during their period of education, and it is also possible that their economic performance is raised at one time but that the extra payment for this is not forthcoming until later.

Of course, the existence of many variables, all of which may influence the economic performance of individuals and between which there may exist many other relationships as well, complicates enormously the problem of discerning the influence of any single variable. The fact that the research problem is difficult, however, does not imply that any one variable, for example, education, makes no contribution at all. Thus, several years ago the proposition that education was productive had a much less secure foundation in empirical research than it has today, but that was not a valid reason then (and it is even less one now) for administrators to ignore the economic impact of education. Even today, empirical research is still in a most primitive condition in the U.K. The most important contribution to measuring the part played by education (Peston, Ziderman and Blaug, 1966) is not all satisfactory and is easily criticised. It would be fallacious, however, to move automatically from criticism and understanding of methodological difficulties to total rejection of the evidence. It would be equally fallacious to postpone automatically certain decisions because the evidence is imperfect.

The multi-variate multi-equation situation exists throughout the study of human behaviour, and in no place is empirical research finished or free from all criticism. It is not easy for administrators to draw the appropriate conclusions, which is that evidence must be evaluated and related to the decisions which have to be taken.

Having argued that the economics of education is of value to the administrator in the first place by the way it formulates problems and its methods of research, it is important to go on, secondly, to consider its substantive empirical contributions. These are as follows:

(a) That having allowed for all the other variables which are likely to influence the distribution of income and having attributed the remaining income difference to education, the value of education in producing income differences may be calculated as a rate of return. This rate of return is typically in the range 6–12 per cent per annum and compares favourably with returns to investment in the public and private sectors. From the point of view of the individual this formulation is adequate. From the national standpoint an additional assumption has to be made, namely, that incomes measure productivities (more strictly, that income differences measure differences in marginal productivities).

(b) Calculations of this kind have been carried out for different levels of education, and show that returns vary between levels. Calculations could be carried out by subject and qualifications acquired but have not yet been brought to any final stage.

(c) Using work of this kind it is possible to calculate what share of a country's growth is attributable to improvements in human capital as opposed simply to the quantity of labour, physical capital and technical progress. As much as fifty per cent of growth is attributable to human capital. At the same time no simple correlation has been found to exist between national growth rates and per cent of national income devoted to education. (This is true of time series analyses of individual countries and cross-section analyses between countries.)

(d) There is a correlation between level of national income per capita and the proportion devoted to education. This is usually interpreted as a demand relationship—the higher is income per head the more education people demand.

All the results mentioned here merit further examination and current research is being carried out on these matters. In particular, reference must be made to the information on education contained in the 1966 census, which the D.E.S. are attempting to supplement with further information on income in order to provide new (and better) estimates of the rate of return to investment on human capital in the U.K.

At this point there are two further matters to be mentioned relating the economy to education. The first concerns a result that has not been established but which many people have been looking for. This is the relationship between the input–output characteristics of particular industrial processes and the educational and training requirements of the labour force. The assumption that there exist simple education–occupation relationships now seems to have been wildly optimistic, and any connection between education and occupation, if it can be discovered, is expected to be extremely complex. Certainly, we cannot look forward in the near future to a system of manpower planning based on a projection of gross national product (even if that is sub-divided by industry) and related via occupational structure to a projection for education and training. This is not to say that manpower planning is unimportant or impossible, but merely that it must proceed on a piecemeal basis and on the assumption that there are many alternative combinations of education and training suitable for any given occupation.

The second matter relates to the cost of education. It is well known that education is labour intensive in the sense that its wage and salary bill is a larger percentage of its total cost than is true of economic activity in general. This means that as gross national product per capita rises, the *same* amount of resources to be used in education will cost more and more. In other words, merely to stand still in terms of inputs we must spend more on education over time. The point may be put in another way as follows; if national income rises by 3 per cent and we spend 3 per cent more on education, thus maintaining the share of expenditure on education in national income, the increase in resources used in education will be less than 3 per cent.

The impact of education on the economy tells the administrator that education does have economic value. Eventually it will provide him with information in sufficient detail to enable him to intervene actively in the education system to achieve economic ends. For the moment, however, the greater contribution of the economist has been in his analysis of problems and his ability to show that things are a good deal more complicated than they appear at first sight. Although this is a fairly limited claim it is worth noting that a proper basis of economic analysis would have avoided some of the more nonsensical conclusions about shortages or surpluses of scientists, doctors and the like contained in various official reports of the past fifteen years; the Jones report on the brain drain would not have had its value so much reduced by faulty calculations of the cost of losing scientists and engineers; and the Robbins report would not have produced such a low estimate of the demand for university places.

Another example of the relevance of economic theory to educational decision-making is connected with the point made earlier about the relative labour intensity of educational processes. What is involved is a rise in the price of labour (i.e. teachers and administrators) relative to the price of capital (equipment, machines, etc.) and a rise in the price of education relative to goods and services in general. In the normal case if prices rise, other things being equal, demand falls. In the case of education we do not know what the price elasticity of demand is, all our knowledge being of income elasticities. This does not mean that we ought not to ask how policy should respond to this relative increase in prices. Moreover, the rise in wages and prices relative to capital costs would suggest, other things being equal, that capital should be substituted for labour in the teaching process. If this is not to happen someone must be obliged to say why not. (The answer that a single fixed pupil ratio is the right one has no basis in theory or fact, just as there is little theory or fact to throw light on the consequences of variations in that ratio.)

I now turn to the role of economics within education. The economist views any organisation as converting resources or inputs into services or outputs. This is a perfectly general formulation and input–output relationships must not be assumed to pertain solely to manufacturing processes. It is not true that this detracts from education in any way, implies that educational institutions should use few resources, or leads to the view that the process of education should be devoted more to the alleged needs of the economy. It does mean that, given the ends of educational institutions, thought might be given to the extent to which these are being achieved efficiently. Economic efficiency means maximisation of the satisfaction of prescribed ends for given resources or minimisation of the use of resources for given degrees of satisfaction of ends. In either formulation it does not matter what the ends as such are.

Now it could be argued that educational institutions are special in the sense that explicit concern with the use of resources is itself detrimental to education. Even if this were always true, we could still engage in exercises to compare, for example, the educational disbenefit of the process of organising teachers' time effectively with the benefit of the better use of that time. In fact, however, nobody has yet shown that deliberate waste of resources within educational institutions has value in education itself.

With this as background the economist's role begins with the desire to have the process of education defined in terms of resource use. What inputs of labour, raw materials (including the pupils themselves specified according to such relevant characteristics as intelligence quotient and socio-economic class), buildings, and capital are used in different educational systems? Can we classify these inputs in such a way that different educational institutions are comparable? Do all educational institutions of the same type use the same structure of inputs? How does the structure of inputs change as the type of institution changes?

A little reflection shows that these last two questions get very close to the problem of the output of educational institutions. Before going on to that, it is important to emphasise the need to take the input side seriously. It is not true that we can make no progress with the study of efficiency without measuring output. It is true at the present time that we still know much too little about resource use within the educational system. The D.E.S. has been working on these matters for a couple of years only, and an entirely satisfactory classification of inputs of the sort mentioned in the previous paragraph is not yet available. The

U.G.C. has also been venturing into the field of the use of staff time, and as a result all the pitfalls involved have been drawn to our notice. Even such a simple question as whether a particular institution is 'cheap' or 'dear' cannot be answered with any confidence except in a trivial budgetary sense.

Let me, however, now turn to the output side. Clearly, educational institutions produce an output in the sense that they achieve something. If we set aside the research aspects of certain specialised institutions, what is produced is the education of the pupils. Starting on the positive side we may identify either in practice or in principle the following components of output:

  (i) The number of pupils at each level within the institution.

  (ii) The abilities of these pupils with respect to easily specifiable activities such as reading, writing, etc.

  (iii) The abilities of these pupils with respect to more complicated skills of perception, organisation, logical deduction, etc.

  (iv) The performance of these pupils in academic examinations.

  (v) The value placed on education by existing pupils.

  (vi) The value placed on education by past pupils.

  (vii) The destination of the pupils (occupation or another educational institution on leaving).

(viii) The interests of the pupils and their free-time activities.

  (ix) The attitudes of the pupils to relevant phenomena as defined by educators and others.

  (x) The external behaviour of pupils, for example, their propensity to be law abiding, socially responsible, etc.

All of these and, perhaps, many other relevant components of educational output may be specified, identified, observed in practice and frequently quantified. It is far from true, therefore, that the output of an educational system is intangible; if by that is meant unspecifiable, unidentifiable, unobservable, non-quantifiable or any combination of the four. We can, therefore, relate these components to variations in the resources used, and test hypotheses about the effects of such variations. All that prevents us is a lack of interest in many quarters, and, for those of us who are interested, a shortage of finance for research.

A typical hypothesis we may want to test is that the substitution of capital for labour in the process of secondary school teaching (i.e. using the same sum of money to hire more teaching machines and fewer teachers) will raise output under components (i)–(iv), but lower it under components (v)–(x). This is what is frequently asserted, and there is no doubt that it can be tested. Any work of this kind must inevitably run into criticism on the grounds that there is more to education than components (i)–(x). Nobody will doubt this; there are many specifiable, or identifiable, or observable, or quantifiable components that the present writer has forgotten or is entirely ignorant of. These present no difficulty in principle. It is suggested, however, that there are certain so-called intangibles which can never be fitted into such categories. In the worst cases (as, for example, in some of the passages of the Crowther and Newsom reports) this amounts to an intangibility of thought on the part of the writers together with what can almost be described as wilful obscurantism and anti-rationalism. Apart from that, and the normal caution and uncertainties involved in all scientific work, it may readily be agreed that there are qualitative aspects of the educational process which are not easily stated in explicit form or describable in ways which make the comparison of different institutions or the same institution at different points of time an easy one. One would not want to reject entirely this notion of quality or attribute it solely to the subjective experience of different observers even though one may be just as struck by their differences as by their agreements. What must be emphasised, however, is that none of these intangibles detract from the possibility of studying input–output relationships between the tangibles, especially as nobody carrying out such a study would ever want to claim more than tentative value for his research or that it told the whole story.

The approach to educational output as a vector (as opposed to a scalar) of many components is of help to the decision-maker. It does not replace him. In a particular case he may still say, for example, that the substitution of machines for teachers changes adversely 'the basic quality of education', and judge this as more than enough to offset any improvements in other components of education. Any study of institutions may be carried out in association with expert judges of the intangibles of education whose reports may be placed alongside the research results. In the final analysis the administrator may revert to the view that there are no input–output relationships and state either that 'there is really one way to educate people' or that 'the inputs themselves determine the nature of the outputs so that there is no output problem at all'. In either case despite the trivialities or circularities involved the economist will have made the administrator face up to certain problems even if his ultimate response is to turn his face away and reject them.

Although it is my view that research (theoretical and empirical) into the output side of the process of education is the most important and exciting activity that currently faces all of us (and not simply the economist), and will eventually be of immense help to the administrator, it would be wrong to ignore three other matters which concern the economist (although again not just him) and dominate the work of the administrator. The first and easiest is one which the D.E.S. is interested in and has provided support for, namely, the finance of education. Research has been undertaken to discover precisely how education is financed, and there has been much debate about alternative methods of finance. Attempts are being made to discover the various sources of finance to the private sector and, in particular, the extent of state subsidies. At the same time questions arise about the role of free education within the maintained system, and what precisely is its justification. Similarly, in recent years student grants have been called into question and some economists have advocated the introduction of loans. In addition, bearing in mind the unrepresentative social class composition of sixth forms, economists like myself have pressed for grants on a large scale to encourage voluntary staying on at school. The assumptions about finance that dominated the reforms from 1870 to 1945, while they are still uppermost in the minds of most educationists are, and must continue to be, called in question.

The next matter I would like to take up is really implicit in everything I have had to say up to now. It is a characteristic of public sector decision-making in the U.K. that it is *ad hoc* and partial. By this I mean that it is frequently a matter of responding to events rather than anticipating and preparing for them, is usually lacking in a basis of empirical knowledge, and is always pursued without due regard to many crucial inter-relationships. The notion of seriously approaching education as an interrelated system which can be planned in a sensible way (i.e. taking account of many alternative possibilities and devising contingency arrangements for the unexpected) has been bruited for a few years and appeared to be accepted by Anthony Crosland, when Secretary of State. It now seems to have gone quite dead although a planning section has been set up at the D.E.S. Even if this assessment is somewhat exaggerated one waits with baited breath to hear what has happened to the National Plan for Education. By this is meant not a single blue-print for the future which would be a strait-jacket and a perpetual embarrass-ment to ministers, but a structure of analysis for decision within which possible alternatives for pupils and teachers at all levels and in all subjects could be compared, the effects of different scales of equipment could be examined, and the consequences of variations in such things as the school leaving age, the length of the academic year, the ratio of general to vocational education, and the value of such things as continuous versus sandwich courses could be explored. To the economist looking in, so to speak, it is difficult at present to discover the rationale for decisions in any of these areas. Instead what he sees is controversy and conflict between what is good or bad in education, on the one hand, and what we can or cannot afford, on the other.

The last matter which the economist might wish to raise concerns the administrator himself. Very little is known about how decisions are actually taken about education in this country, and even less is put forward to justify the present decision structure from D.E.S. at the one extreme through to the head-mistress of an infant school (or, dare I say, the head of a univer-sity department) at the other. What is the theoretical basis for what exists at present? Is there any evidence that the present structure is more efficient than an alternative one?

Bibliography

Becker, G.S. (1964) *Human Capital*, Princeton, N.J.: Princeton University Press.

Bowen, W.G. (1964) *Economic Aspects of Education*, Princeton, N.J.: Princeton University Press.

Mushkin, S.J. (ed.) (1962) *Economics of Higher Education*, Washington, D.C.: Department of Health, Education and Welfare.

Parnes, H.S. (ed.) (1963) *Planning Education for Economic and Social Development*, Paris: O.E.C.D.

Peston, M., Ziderman, A. and Blaug, M. (1967) *The Utilisation of Educated Manpower in Industry*, Edinburgh and London: Oliver and Boyd.

Robinson, E.A.G. and Vaizey, J.E. (eds.) (1966) *The Economics of Education: Proceedings of a Conference of the International Economic Association*, London: Macmillan.

Chapter 5

Role Theory and Educational Administration

Peter S. Burnham

In the developing field of administrative theory, resulting in the main from the contributions of American social scientists working in a variety of organisational settings, the importance of role theory as a 'tool of analysis' has been increasingly recognised. While not yet fully fledged and clearly defined (Biddle and Thomas, 1966), it has shown itself capable of throwing a good deal of light on the behaviour of people in the educational field, from teachers and deputy heads to principals and local authority administrators.

The concept of role has been widely used in the larger field of organisational theory (Hoyle, 1965). Institutions, such as colleges and schools, are organised agencies designed to carry out specialised tasks for the social system. Any organisational group facing a common task or problem will experience the need for certain identifiable functions to be performed. Rather than leave the performance of these behaviours to chance—as in the informal group—they are combined into separate 'offices' and arranged in some form of organisational structure of positions. Institutional behaviour, then, may be thought of as being organised around offices or positions which are compounded of the various functions and behaviours vital to the well-being and purposes of the organisation.

These positions are collections of rights and duties, distinguished from one another, and designated by a title such as principal, deputy head or teacher. Other symbols of identification include dress or badge of rank, and the physical setting within which the incumbent operates: the teacher in his classroom, the caretaker in his boiler-room or the head in his study with a name-plate on the door. Positions are also defined by the social and educational attributes required to occupy the position (middle class values, a degree, wide experience, a teaching

72

certificate); by psychological characteristics such as temperament or intelligence; and by the relationship to other people or
positions (Oeser and Harary, 1962). Within the organisation,
positions are ordered hierarchically in terms of status, and may
be thought of as locations on an organisational chart.

Associated with every position in an organisation is a set of
expectations concerning what is appropriate behaviour for a
person occupying that position, and these 'appropriate behaviours' comprise the role associated with the office. In order to
differentiate these two terms—position and role—one might say
that a person *occupies* a position but *plays* or *performs* a role
(Levinson, 1959). A role is the dynamic aspect of a position
(Linton, 1952).

Each role incumbent is expected to perform certain kinds of
functions, and to act in certain specific and differentiated ways in
his relations with the persons with whom he interacts. For a
head, these include pupils, parents, teachers and other heads.[1]
The concepts of role and role expectation thus provide one way
of thinking about administrative behaviour. In this sense,
administration can be seen as the process of defining, allocating
and integrating roles and personnel to maximise the probability
of achieving the goals of the organisation (Hills, 1960). Clearly,
the role expectations must be oriented towards such ends. It
is these normative behavioural expectations which represent the
institutional (or what has been called the nomothetic) dimension
of behaviour within an organisation (Getzels, 1963).

The role is linked with the position and not with the person
who is only 'temporarily' occupying that position. However,
as each person occupying a position brings his own individual
personality to bear on the role, actual role performance may be
thought of as a fusion of role expectations and 'self'.[2] In this
way, as Getzels (1958) points out, each individual stamps the
particular role he plays with the unique style of his own personality. Hence, while *what* one is expected to do is prescribed,

[1] Throughout this chapter, illustrations will be largely concerned with the role
of the headmaster. There is no intention, however, to limit the relevance of role
theory to this one position; the head is used as one example from a whole range of
administrators in the field of education.

[2] Sarbin (1954) defines 'self' as the organisation of qualities (traits, attitudes,
habits, personal skills) and need-dispositions (sentiments and drives).

how one actually plays the role will be distinguished by personal nuances. So, just as the institution can be defined by positions, roles and role expectations, individuals can be defined by their personalities and need-dispositions. This personal aspect of an organisation is referred to as the idiographic dimension.[1]

It is obvious that administrators need to take both role and personality into account when allocating persons to positions within the organisation, if they are to deal with the factors which contribute to conflict, efficiency and job-satisfaction. It is far more than a once-and-for-all fitting of round pegs into round holes, for the playing of a role is both dynamic and creative.

If they are to maximise the staffing potential within the institution and create an organisation that is both efficient and effective, administrators need to encourage the creative fusion of personality and role among their staff, to reinforce those personality attributes which enhance the roles particular individuals are playing, and to make wise 'marriages' between personalities and positions. Effectiveness can be held to relate to the co-operative achievement of organisational goals and is thus institutional and non-personal in character; efficiency can be held to relate to the satisfaction of individual needs and is personal in character (Barnard, 1938). It is the function of the administrator to secure the right balance between these two dimensions; it is not sufficient that he concerns himself with nomothetic considerations alone. As Westwood (1966) has pointed out, neither the nomothetic leader (the tough bureaucratic boss) stressing institutional requirements, procedures and rules, nor the idiographic leader (the easy going head whose paramount concern is the contentment of his staff) emphasising the interests, needs and personalities of the staff, is necessarily appropriate. What seems to be required is the 'transactional' leader, who achieves and maintains the necessary equilibrium in the organisation (Getzels, Lipham and Campbell, 1968). In a large school, for example, this may be the function of the total *leadership situation* towards which a number of positions will be contributing (the deputy head, senior mistress, housemasters, heads of departments, and so on, as well as the head).

---

[1] For a discussion of the nomothetic and idiographic dimensions of an organisation, see Getzels (1963).

A major part of the administrator's job is to stake out the differentiated roles of the staff in such a way as to make the best match between institutional demands and staff personality needs (Campbell, 1964b). Who is to take 4c and who 1a? Who is to be careers master and who the year master of the first form? In a college of education who should be nominated as chairman of the academic review board, who upgraded as senior woman tutor to deal with the students' personal problems, and who selected as co-ordinator of the professional studies? As schools and colleges become bigger and more complex, differentiation of function increases, calling for further role specification. What used to be done by one person is now a job for two or three. Administrators need periodically to re-define the roles in a changing institution, to expand certain roles to cover behavioural gaps in the task structure, to be aware of role confusion or role ambiguity, and to arbitrate in cases of dispute over role demarcation.

In these days of social change, educational innovation and school re-organisation, there is a recurring need for the educational administrator to be both vigilant and sensitive regarding the role fabric of his school or college organisation. For instance, the introduction of ancillary staff into schools has led to the increased interaction of professional and artisan roles (science master and lab technician; games master and groundsman; duty teacher and dinner lady), heightening the possibility of role conflict in the institution. The introduction of auxiliary staff into schools on a greater scale than at present (teachers' aides and part-time helpers) and the possible differentiation of the teaching force itself into generalists and specialists or in the team teaching situations associated with inter-disciplinary enquiry, may create many new and delicate role definition problems for the head. Often there is little or no tradition to help in these matters.

Campbell notes that specialist positions within the large school have highly differentiated roles and the incumbents tend to perceive the organisation in the light of their own discriminative needs, interests and knowledge. The sixth form physics master may have little interest in, or patience with, the needs and problems of the teacher of the slow learners; or the French

75

expert in his language laboratory with the concerns of the non-graduate careers master grappling with the vocational aspirations of the lower streams. Instead of dealing with fairly diffuse and generalised roles among which teachers are easily interchangeable—as in the primary school or the old elementary school—the secondary school head is challenged with finding ways of understanding and utilising dozens of specialists, with defining their roles, and with mediating the bird's-nest tangle of differing and often conflicting expectations. Increased school size supports a more complex division of labour, bringing into the school a more heterogeneous array of highly trained specialists who desire and are competent to exercise independent judgment within their realms of expertise (Charters, 1964). Yet these very same forces increase the necessity of delimiting the autonomy of such persons in the interests of co-ordination. The resolution of this dilemma is one of the important challenges confronting the educational administrator. Role specification, or the outlining in detail of the rights, privileges and responsibilities of each position, and role co-ordination, are major organisational tasks.

A changing school environment demands a changing school (Herriott and St. John, 1966). The change from grammar school to comprehensive school—from a clientele largely aspiring towards middle class values to one including a sizeable proportion with working class values—necessitates more than a change of methods and procedures. The teachers need to take on new role elements; to adjust their attitudes and expectations; and to re-formulate their objectives and approaches. The head must diagnose the changing needs of the pupils and effect the necessary adjustments to the role structure of the school, leading the teachers to understand and accept a new interpretation of their role. And because schools are embedded in a culture with both local and national orientations, it is essential that the roles created shall be consonant with a wide spectrum of social and individual needs.

The genius of administration, according to Nolte (1966), lies in this endless process of diagnosing, defining, classifying and interpreting roles, in the context of an intimate knowledge of the personalities of a large and varied staff. It is a competency which requires to be based on a clear understanding of the social and educational goals of the institution, a thorough analysis of the jobs to be done, and a perceptive awareness of the interests, skills and idiosyncrasies of the staff.

II

A role, then, is concerned with what a person does, whereas role expectations consist of shared attitudes held by persons defining the role—attitudes about what a role occupant should or should not do (Lieberman, 1956). However, it is not the formal system alone which sets up role expectations; individuals and groups within the informal system also play a considerable part. As the teachers interact with one another in the gossip groupings of the staffroom, as they meet in their friendship groups at social evenings and in their homes outside school, as they knock up against one another in the daily routine of school life, so the pointed comments and asides build up a climate of expectations about colleagues. It is a commonplace of the organisational scene to talk about 'the old man'. Turner (1962) has said that the formalised roles are to the full roles as detonators to explosives, merely devices to set them off. This is particularly true of those roles which involve close and/or friendly contact with the staff, parents or children, such as the head, the deputy head, the school secretary and the school counsellor. The administrator is thus not the only person who defines roles in the institution, though he may be the first and the most decisive.

Three important factors can be said to have relevance for the structure of role expectations. First, apprehension of the expectations of others, awareness of just how one is supposed to behave, will depend on the role incumbent's perceptual acuity and accuracy (Argyle, 1952; Brookover, 1955). The finer points of a role definition may be acquired only by a perceptually sophisticated person able to 'read' the fleeting or esoteric cues and gestures: the smile, the pause, the significance of the raised eyebrow, the meaningful absence of a member of staff, and such subtle responses to one's first tentative steps in the role. Each tiny cue and response acts as a gentle shaper of the role incumbent's behaviour. At first, only the iceberg-tip of a role pre-

77

scription will be spelled out; at the interview for the job, during the initial briefing sessions, and in the duty rostas and standing orders on the staff notice-board. A few salient 'boundary-stones' will be set out, the rest being left for the individual to find out in more informal ways; this 'filling-in' stage being high on the list of priorities for the newcomer to any organisation. In some cases, helping the new member of staff to fit in may be a responsibility attached to the role of the deputy head as social-emotional leader of the informal system; in others, it may be carried out even more informally by an experienced and friendly colleague.

It is at this stage that the administrator must be aware of the significance of his own behaviour to a newcomer eager to do the right thing, in that his every gesture and response will be analysed for clues as to his degree of approval or disapproval. For a head to forget to greet a young teacher with his first name, or to fail to notice him when passing in the corridor, may be enough to trigger off in the young teacher a long and searching review of his recent role behaviour. The head, himself, should also be concerned to 'read' the responses of his staff to ascertain whether he is meeting their expectations for administration or leadership.

Second, the intensity or narrowness with which an expectation is defined will range from 'strongly required' or 'must' at one end of the continuum, to 'prohibited' or 'must not' at the other, with an indeterminate area of tolerated or openly permissive behaviour in between (Levinson, 1959). For instance, the head may be strongly required by the teachers to keep parents away from the classrooms; the teachers may be strongly required by the head to leave the staffroom when the bell rings; parents may be prohibited from entering school premises; and the teachers' code may require that they must not criticise a colleague in the presence of other staff or children. About these more extreme role prescriptions, there will usually be little doubt. However, the teacher might experience considerable difficulty in determining whether he may or may not (as *he* pleases) wear a bright red shirt to school, join the local Labour club, teach with his coat off, or smoke as he goes about the school; the head as to whether he may or may not (as *he* pleases) go into the staffroom for a chat on other than formal occasions, be an irregular church-goer, or decline to participate in local community affairs. In all such cases, the newcomer will need to explore his role in a very chary 'now I am warm, now I am cold' way.

The third important factor having relevance for the structure of role expectations, is the role incumbent's perceptions of the legitimacy or illegitimacy of the expectations of others to which he is exposed. Gross, Mason and McEachern (1958) define a legitimate expectation as one which the incumbent of a position feels others have a right to hold. At one time, if the principal and staff of a teacher training college held strong expectations for the personal and social behaviour of the students, an example of which might be the requirement that they be in their beds with lights out by a fixed time in the evening, these were perceived as legitimate by the students of the day. Now, in a different social climate, such expectations would be rejected as illegitimate by most students and seen as a violation of their personal freedom. In the same way, headteachers sometimes require certain responses from their staff that may not be construed as legitimate by the staff. In one school, the head strongly required the men teachers to wear a suit with the middle button done up, much to the dismay and annoyance of a number of young teachers who did not concede that this was a legitimate expectation. In a changing society, there is obviously considerable scope here for conflict and dissatisfaction among staff. Even changes in teaching methods may give rise to difficulties of this kind; for instance, certain teachers who have grown up with the belief that 'pedagogic isolation' is a right may feel that it is illegitimate to be expected to teach with other teachers present, as in team-teaching.

To the extent that the role incumbent conforms to the expectations for his position, so he permits the other people with whom he interacts to anticipate his behaviour. In this way, he enables them to respond adequately. Roles are complementary and interdependent, in that each and every role derives its meaning from other related roles in the organisation. What is seen as a 'right' for one role may be prescribed as an 'obligation' for a related role; and conversely, the 'obligation' of one role may be the 'right' of a colleague. Rights may be thought of as the behaviours 'due' to the role incumbent; obligations the behaviours he 'owes' to the occupants of related positions. To the extent that he meets with the expectations directed at him, so the rights associated with his role will be accorded; to the extent that he fails to meet with the expectations, so his rights will be withdrawn (Lieberman, 1956). In this sense, the role behaviours of related positions act as role sanctions for the individual. As we have already noted, should the head of a school fail to meet with the legitimate expectations of the teachers, examples of which might be the requirement that he consults them over important matters or sets an acceptable tone for the school, then the teachers may decide to disavow some of their obligations towards the head and withdraw their support for his policies. They may decide to 'work to rule' and carry out only the mandatory behaviours. It can be seen from this that a head's authority really lies in the teachers' evaluations of his behaviour; the head must clearly earn his authority. Bates (1957) states that it is the anticipatory nature of role reciprocity which enables the interacting individuals in an organisation to articulate their roles, and to function collectively as an integrated unit.

III

Any individual will have a whole series of role relationships based on the many roles he plays in society. In addition to his professional role, the headmaster may also play the roles of husband, father, uncle, lay preacher, examiner, secretary to the local tennis club, freemason, and so on. This collection of roles Merton (1957a) called the 'status-set', and it is clear that these multiple roles can present many problems of compromise and co-ordination. The head may find it difficult to reconcile the competing role expectations for his behaviour associated with the widely different positions he occupies. As a professional person, he will give precedence to the occupational role, but this may still leave him with role problems. If he lives in the school community, he may find that he is expected to take on various 'outside' roles conditional upon his being head of the school, such as those of church elder or chairman of the fete committee. It is for this reason that some headteachers withdraw completely from the local community in order to compartmentalise the role of the head, and limit the strain resulting from too extensive a repertoire for the role.

However, with regard solely to his professional position, the administrator will be involved in a whole series of role relationships (Southall, 1959). His position might be visualised as at the centre of a web of relationships, a pattern referred to by Merton (1957b) as the 'role-set'. For the head of a school, the role-set would include the director of education, the inspectorate, the staff of the school (though here one might easily find the staff divided into several 'audience groups'), the caretaker, the deputy head, the school secretary, the children, the parents, the governors and the community as a whole through its various committees and pressure groups.

Obviously, some expectations are more directly and importantly involved than others; some will come from superiors and some from subordinates; some from people with whom the head is in constant touch and some from those in peripheral positions. The basic problem is one of integrating the role expectations of all the members of the role-set. It is clear that there exists in the role-set a considerable potential for differing, conflicting and, sometimes, quite incompatible role expectations. Gross, Mason and McEachern (1958) found that superintendents of schools were faced with conflicting expectations from parents, teachers and school boards. In a study of the role of the deputy head, Burnham (1964) discovered that heads and teachers were perceived as holding quite contrary expectations for the deputy head's role. The heads were perceived by the deputy head as wanting him to engage in behaviour concerned with school organisation, such as timetable making or assigning teachers to school duties, while the teachers were perceived as wanting him to carry out behaviours manifesting concern for them, such as listening to their problems or relaying their suggestions to the head.

This last study shows that the concept of role is further complicated by the fact that the expectations are not necessarily simple and direct in form. What counts is not only what teachers, governors, parents and others in the role-set *really* expect of the head, or what they *say* they expect, but what the head *perceives* them to be expecting—a fact which is often at the bottom of many of the misunderstandings that occur in organisations. It is at this point, also, that the possibility exists of 'perceptual seduction' in that factors such as power, high status, propinquity, affiliation and the threat of sanctions, may 'persuade' the role incumbent to perceive one set of expectations as being more legitimate than another, irrespective of any objective importance or relevance. The administrator is constantly faced with the difficulty of assessing the legitimacy of expectations, and the relative weightings which are to be given to different sets of expectations, and he must be vigilant in guarding against perceptual distortion.

There is also the complication that the concept of role has to be considered from three different points of view (Levinson, 1959). First of all, in the sense that we have already been discussing it, are the *role demands* emanating from the role-set which seek to channel, guide, support, adjust and prescribe the behaviour of a position. Second, there is the individual's own inner definition of the role or *role conception*, what he personally and ideally thinks he ought to do. Third, there is the actual *role performance* or observed behaviours resulting from the interaction of the role demands, the individual's role conception and the characteristics of his personality. Many deputy heads, after adjusting their role performance to meet the perceived role demands of their headteachers, found that their greatest source of conflict lay in the disparity between this actual role behaviour and their ideal conception of the role (Burnham, 1964). It is at this point that we realise how great is the propensity for conflict in any role, but particularly for those with a wide and varied role-set, such as that faced by the administrator of a large institution.

The leadership role in schools and colleges is particularly vulnerable to role conflict. Perhaps the simplest kind of conflict situation, and certainly the one viewed most apprehensively by the administrator, is that between role expectations and personality (Getzels, 1963). Many aspiring teachers must have wondered if they were going to be able to live up to the role expectations associated with the job of head. The primary aim of most interviewing committees would seem to be that of selecting on the basis of personality relative to the needs of 'leadership'. In some organisations, quite elaborate personality tests and structured situations are used to select those most fitted temperamentally and psychologically for the top jobs. Yet the trait approach to leadership has been shown to be inadequate and unproven. Studies of leaders in different situations have failed to discover any particular syndrome of personality traits that regularly characterise such individuals and differentiate clearly between leaders and non-leaders (Stogdill, 1948; Gibb, 1954). This does not mean, of course, that personal qualities are not relevant to the administrator role. Clearly, administrative style is likely to depend a good deal on personality.

The possibility that personality may conflict with role expectations in the school can be seen when one imaginatively considers the case of the gentle natured, easy-going head of a small village school suddenly promoted into a bigger and tougher urban school, being forced by the situational expectations to adopt a tough-minded, more authoritarian manner. If one looks at the role of the teacher, it is possible to sympathise with the rather traditional and authoritarian old-timer trying to 'maintain standards' in a school de-streamed by a new and permissive headmaster.

Lipham (1960) showed that principals of schools were expected to exert themselves energetically, to strive for higher status, and to relate themselves successfully to other people—situations requiring high levels of drive, social ability, mobility and emotional control. The study suggested that persons having a basic personality structure characterised by such needs and dispositions would suffer less strain in fulfilling the head's role.

Psychologically distant heads of task groups were shown by Fiedler (1960) to be more effective than heads who tend towards warmer and psychologically closer relations with subordinates. He maintains that it is for this reason that in large organisations intercourse between leaders and followers is limited by an elaborate system of rules and institutionalised barriers (Fiedler, 1957). In a school or college, these might include such things as a separate toilet for the head, separate arrangements for tea-

83

breaks, a personal study distant from the staffroom, a secretary to 'bar the way', a rule or understanding that the head is only available to staff at certain times, and a notice-board for the head's communications. Fiedler goes on to point out that while it is commonly thought that these barriers exist to prevent subordinates becoming too familiar with the head, they primarily serve to protect the head from emotional involvement with the staff. The leader is then less likely to have the opportunity to form close friendships which could lead to favouritism towards some and poor discipline among the rest. Should he do so, he would find it difficult to reach unpopular decisions uninfluenced by his feelings. An emotionally dependent head is easily exploited by his staff.

It would seem that an administrator must choose whether he is to fulfill his own individual personality needs or the institutional requirements of his role. To try to satisfy both is to increase the possibility of role strain. However, if he chooses simply to indulge his own needs, he is likely to be an unsatisfactory administrator and thus fail to meet the expectations of the role-set; if he chooses to fulfill the requirements of his role to the letter, he may well be frustrated personally. In his study of school executives, Seeman (1960) concludes that there is a danger that heads may come to be alienated from their staff (and often from themselves as persons), for 'to the leader we seem to offer position and advancement at a minimum cost of isolation'.[1]

If we examine a second major type of conflict situation, we shall find that a good deal of the conflict in the leadership role is rooted in the norms and values of society. These cultural imperatives impose mutually conflicting demands with which institutional leadership must deal (Seeman, 1953). First, there is the conflict between the success ideology and the equality ideology, whether in relation to staff or pupils. On the one hand, the head is expected to stress competition, differentiation of

---

[1] Anyone who has regularly visited schools as an 'informed outsider' will have sensed and experienced the professional and psychological hunger of many lonely heads, eager for some confirmation of their ideas, for some sympathy with their disenchantment over young teachers' attitudes, and, very often, for sheer human friendship and conversation.

84

staff and pupils, rank orders and mark-lists, job techniques, rewards and punishments, talk about the job, and task goals; on the other hand, to emphasise shared feelings, mutual support, friendship groupings, personal interests and social functions.

Second, there is the conflict between the needs for dependence and independence. While some teachers are submissive and like to be told what to do, others demand more independence, initiative and personal responsibility. But as we have seen, too much autonomy among teachers in a large school can give rise to problems of control and co-ordination for the head.

Third, the head is often faced with the choice between *universalistic* as against *particularistic* criteria for his behaviour. As a key figure in the distribution of resources and sanctions, the head must operate from a universalistic frame of reference, in that he must treat everyone alike, be seen to be fair and just, and have no personal favourites. If the school is to avoid having 'blue-eyed boys', 'inner cabinets' and 'creepers', the head must renounce too intimate ties with his staff. Much as the head might like to assess and relate to members of staff in particularistic terms, as 'friends', he is forced to judge them according to such universalistic criteria as professional qualifications and job competence. Getzels (1952) suggests that in large bureaucratic organisations, the allocations of roles is made according to universalistic criteria, and not, as in very small schools, on more personal grounds. With the bureaucratisation of comprehensive schools, the trend is likely to be towards universalistic principles of organisation which may involve heart-searching conflict situations for the head, as in taking old Tom off the important examination work because he is so out of date, or in giving the headship of an expanding department to a young newcomer over the heads of two or three established old-timers.[1]

One might also point to the conflict that exists between the motivation of the staff, requiring warm and encouraging support, and their organisation for work and assessment for promotion or report, requiring a cool objectivity and differentiation based on job performance (Wilson, 1962). These two aspects are similar to the two main leader-behaviour factors

[1] For further discussion of these 'pattern variables' or dilemmas of choice see Parsons, 1951 and 1956; and Laulicht, 1955.

teased out by Halpin and Winer (1957) from the Ohio State University Leader Behaviour studies. (See also Stogdill, Scott and Jaynes, 1956; Stogdill and Shartle, 1955.) They suggested that 'initiating structure', or behaviours indicating that the leader was organising, defining roles and establishing new ways of getting things done, and 'consideration', or behaviours indicative of warmth, friendship and mutual trust in the relationship between the leader and his staff, accounted for 83 per cent of the total leader behaviour variance. These two leadership roles seem to be linked to the two major goals of any organisation, namely, goal achievement and group maintenance. It is suggested that specialists in these functions emerge, one the task leader and the other the social-emotional leader (Cartwright and Zander, 1960).

In his study of the role of the deputy head in secondary schools, Burnham (1968) suggests that the leadership role in a large school might be divided into its instrumental and expressive aspects, the head concentrating on the task functions while the deputy head fulfils the social-emotional leadership role. In a large organisation, for a number of cogent reasons, such as the very different personality attributes required for each of these two specialist roles and the increasing amount of time needing to be spent on each area of behaviour, these two aspects of leadership are basically incompatible. However, the two leaders can constitute a dominant or central pair, supporting each other, and dividing between them the performance of the behaviours needed for leadership in the instrumental and expressive areas of the organisation (Bales and Slater, 1956). It would seem that the administration of schools and colleges would be much improved if there was a greater realisation and awareness of the functional aspects of such a leadership alliance.[1]

In a very large school, both the instrumental and expressive functions of the leadership role may be further differentiated, certain elements of each being delegated to other senior members of staff. The instrumental function might be divided between the head and a 'procedural' deputy responsible for

[1] Bales (1955) and Parsons (1954) both point to the functional similarity of the leadership alliance in the organisation and the incest taboo in the nuclear family as socialising mechanisms.

detailed organisation; while the expressive function might be shared by a number of people, including the deputy head, the senior mistress, the housemasters, and the school counsellor. (It would seem that the title of deputy head is rapidly becoming obsolescent when leadership is viewed in this functional way.) The extension of the leadership role into a more complicated leadership pattern involving several senior administrators, does not alter the basic principle that all concerned should form a co-operating and supportive leadership coalition.

Lastly in the field of role conflict, there is the conflict which results from the clash of divergent expectations from members of the role-set. Seeman (1953) highlighted the clash between those expectations of teachers for the administrator which stressed the instrumental aspects of his role, and those which emphasised the expressive aspects. In his study of Ohio school superintendents, Seeman showed that those superintendents who were most successful in securing salary increases for the teachers—and one can assume that this is a permanent expectation—were described by these same teachers as men who did not spend enough time in personal contact with them. The superintendents were perceived as 'stand-offish'. With a limited amount of time at his disposal, the administrator may have to decide whether to carry out the instrumental functions of his role or engage in expressive contact with his staff.

A number of situations come to mind manifesting divergent sets of role expectations for the head. The young teachers on a staff may expect the head to delegate responsibility and encourage innovation, whereas the old guard may want him to leave them alone and maintain the traditions of the past. There will be those on the staff who stress to the head the importance of informal activities, such as school outings and concerts, much to the annoyance of those who want the school to concentrate on the formal task of preparing children for examinations and vocational requirements. Some teachers may expect the head to visit their classrooms to see what is going on, and to offer help and advice, while others would rather he left them alone, trusting them as professional people. In a college of education setting, one can see that the principal may be expected to emphasise academic education by some of the staff and by the university boards of studies, but by others on the staff and by the representatives of practising teachers in the schools to stress practical teaching and classroom know-how.

IV

Finally, we might differentiate between the 'leadership' and 'administrative' aspects in the role of the administrator of an organisation (Lipham, 1964). While these behaviours are different in orientation, they are, nevertheless, integral parts of a broadly conceived administrator-role, and both aspects are concerned with the achievement of the goals and objectives of the institution. As Taylor points out in Chapter 6, the head of a school '...not only administers but also makes policy—sometimes with only a minimum of consultation with those most likely to be affected'—and needs to develop an '...understanding of how educational objectives are defined and the means whereby resources may be organised to achieve them'.

We have seen that 'leadership' is associated with those behaviours which are concerned with initiating new structure and procedures within the organisation for accomplishing or changing the goals of the institution. It is an important part of the head's job to diagnose the needs of the school and to identify new educational objectives. In this role as a 'leader', the head would be carrying out the functions of an innovator. In that sense, he would be playing a role that is somewhat disruptive of the *status quo*.

When the administrator is emphasising the 'administrative' aspect of his role, he will be concerned with making use of existing structure and procedures to achieve the goals of the institution. He concentrates upon maintaining and strengthening rather than changing the established arrangements within the organisation. Hence, in his role as an 'administrator' the head is a stabilising force, a traditionalist, and in that sense, a 'conformist'.

We can now see that the 'administrative-leadership' dimension gives rise to a basic paradox in the role of the head of an organisation. At one time, as Lipham puts it, he must wear an 'administrative hat', and at other times, a 'leadership hat'—

the expectations for his behaviour on many occasions seeming to be quite self-contradictory. Having but one head, he has to be aware of which hat he *is* wearing and, in the context of the situational needs of the organisation, he must decide which hat he *should* be wearing, a decision that clearly requires very great understanding and insight. He must judge when it is more appropriate to move towards change and development, and when it is more politic to integrate changes and consolidate the organisation. To play the role of leader too long, or too often can be dysfunctional for the organisation in that it is likely to impose too great a strain. It is in the making of such decisions that one distinguishes the wise administrator.

It follows, then, that it is for the administrator to determine when he should 'administrate' and when he should 'lead'. The extent to which he carries out these two functions will be determined by his diagnosis and assessment of the school and its task in the social setting. The situation may well vary from term to term. The introduction of comprehensive schools, the up-surge of curriculum reform, the awareness of new vocational and parental expectations, and the recruitment of new members of staff, will all necessitate change in the institution. At such times, a good deal of leadership will be expected of the head.

In defining their concept of *executive professional leadership*, Gross and Herriott (1965) consider that the head needs to keep up with current thinking and research as the intellectual leader of the school; to study the latest methods of teaching, and to work closely with the staff to effect curriculum innovation, as the pedagogic leader of the school; while as educational leader his chief function is to identify problems, co-ordinate the various aspects of new ventures in the school, and consult with individual teachers and groups of teachers regarding their problems.

Whereas leadership may be required only on occasions, administration is a constant requirement. As an administrator, the head is responsible for managing a largely professionally staffed organisation, and for operating a rationally contrived set of arrangements whereby problems can be discovered and discussed, and decisions made. Amongst other duties, he will be responsible for planning, organising, directing, co-ordinating,

89

communicating, decision-making, budgeting, reporting, allocating resources and evaluating (Gulick and Urwick, 1966; Gregg, 1957; Griffiths, Hemphill *et al.*, 1961). In carrying out such duties, he will need to relate to such people as inspectors and organisers, school health service personnel, officials at county hall, school meals staff, the caretaker and the school secretary, local bigwigs, publishers' representatives and so on. Not surprisingly, the teachers on his staff will often feel that he has little or no time for them.

In this respect, Nolte (1966) suggests that many heads become 'wrapped in the embrace of the office'. They become over-concerned with attendance sheets and mark-lists, stationery and supplies, ringing the bell on time, checking dinner money accounts, writing letters to each other, looking over buildings with men from the architect's department, discussing the use of the school hall with the secretary of the local women's guild, and drawing up detailed schemes and standing orders which few have time to read. (See also Katz, 1955.) As the staffroom cynic would put it, there is real danger that the head will become a glorified clerk and tea-brewer.

In the past, it is true, many heads have overstressed the administrative function of their role. Holing-up in their studies for long periods of time, busying themselves with petty routine and simple clerical duties, they have tended to let the school organisation run itself. In discussing superintendents of schools, Halpin (1966) considers that far too many of them allow their main responsibilities to become obscured by trivia, with the result that they abdicate the leadership role and degenerate into mere functionaries. Leadership and innovation generate costs for members of staff and give rise to increased tension and conflict within the organisation. This, in turn, creates anxieties and problems for the head, as the negative affect and annoyance is directed his way. It is tempting to seek the quiet life, to avoid the dilemmas of leadership, by a retreat into 'busywork' and perfunctory activity. The situation is often rationalised by heads as that of a contented staff ticking over quite happily, getting on with the age-old task of educating the pupils, when it is perfectly clear to the outsider that the school has got into a rut and needs a thoroughly good shake-up. This is a process that all too often has to await the appointment of a new head, thus establishing a 'shake-up cycle' for schools of a generation long. For some reason, conflict is construed as 'bad' by many headteachers and principals, when it might more rationally be perceived as the healthy concomitant of innovation and change. Generally speaking, it might be thought that there is too little conflict as a result of leadership in our schools.

It is now clear that the occupants of top positions in educational institutions will need to place much less reliance on experience *per se*, and much more on acquiring the understanding and insight that comes from a conceptual grasp of the nature of their own role, and those of their staff (Campbell, 1964a). So far, principals of colleges and heads of schools have not received adequate professional preparation for their positions. It would seem sensible to include in their training, at some stage, a grasp and understanding of role theory insofar as it illuminates the work of the administrator.

The training of high school principals in techniques of administration is receiving a good deal of attention in the U.S.A. Hughes (1967) concludes his article on the subject of training in school management for headteachers in this country with the assertion that we would do well to introduce our school administrators to the study of administrative theory, with its new emphasis on the insight to be obtained from the social sciences. Lonsdale (1964) suggests that by analysing and studying their own role, and the role structure of the organisation, the administrator can reduce the amount of role conflict within the institution, and help staff to become more sensitive and responsive to others' rights through a better understanding of the nature of their roles. This more rational view of one's job, and of the structure of the educational organisation, is essential if our large schools and colleges are to be adaptive and responsive to the needs of a changing society.

References

Argyle, Michael (1952) 'The Concepts of Role and Status', *The Sociological Review*, **44**, 39–52.
Bales, Robert F. (1955) 'The Equilibrium Problem in Small Groups', in A.

Hare, Edgar Borgatta and Robert F. Bales (eds.) *Small Groups: Studies in Social Interaction*, New York: Alfred Knopf.

Bales, Robert F. and Slater, P.E. (1956) 'Role Differentiation in Small Decision-making Groups', in Talcott Parsons and Robert F. Bales (eds.) *Family: Socialization and Interaction Process*, London: Routledge and Kegan Paul.

Barnard, Chester I. (1938) *The Functions of the Executive*, Cambridge, Mass.: Harvard University Press.

Bates, Frederick L. (1957) 'A Conceptual Analysis of Group Structure', *Social Forces*, **36**, 103.

Biddle, Bruce J. and Thomas, Edwin, J. (1966) *Role Theory: Concepts and Research*, New York: Wiley.

Brookover, W.B. (1955) 'Research on Teacher and Administrator Roles', *Journal of Educational Sociology*, **29**, 2–13.

Burnham, Peter S. (1964) *The Role of the Deputy Head in Secondary Schools*, unpublished M.Ed. thesis, University of Leicester.

Burnham, Peter S. (1968) 'The Deputy Head', in Bryan Allen (ed.) *Head-teachers for the Seventies*, Oxford: Blackwell.

Campbell, Roald F. (1964a) 'The Superintendent—His Role and Professional Status', *Teachers' College Record*, as quoted in M. Chester Nolte (ed.) *An Introduction to School Administration: Selected Readings*, New York: Macmillan, pp. 308–17.

Campbell, Roald F. (1964b) 'Implications for the Practice of Administration', in Daniel E. Griffiths (ed.) *Behavioural Science and Educational Administration*, Chicago: University of Chicago Press, ch. XIII.

Cartwright, Dorwin and Zander, Alvin (1960) 'Leadership and Group Performance', in *Group Dynamics: Research and Theory*, London: Tavistock Publications, 2nd. edn.

Charters, W.W. (1964) 'An Approach to the Formal Organization of the School', in Daniel E. Griffiths (ed.) op. cit., ch. XI.

Chase, Francis S. and Guba, Egon G. (1955) 'Administrative Roles and Behaviour', *Review of Educational Research*, **25**.

Fiedler, Fred E. (1957) 'A Note on Leadership Theory: the Effect of Social Barriers between Leaders and Followers', *Sociometry*, **20**, 87.

Fiedler, Fred E. (1958) *Leader Attitudes and Group Effectiveness*, Urbana, Ill.: University of Illinois Press, p. 44.

Fiedler, Fred E. (1960) 'The Leader's Psychological Distance and Group Effectiveness', in Dorwin Cartwright and Alvin Zander (eds.) op. cit.

Getzels, Jacob W. (1952) 'A Psycho-Sociological Framework for the Study of Educational Institutions', *Harvard Educational Review*, **22**, 234–46.

Getzels, Jacob W. (1958) 'Administration as a Social Process' in Andrew W. Halpin (ed.) *Administrative Theory in Education*, Chicago: Midwest Administrative Center, University of Chicago, pp. 153–5.

Getzels, Jacob W. (1963) 'Conflict and Role Behaviour in the Educational Setting', in W.W. Charters and N.L. Gage (eds.) *Readings in the Social Psychology of Education*, Boston: Allyn and Bacon, p. 309.

Getzels, Jacob W., Lipham, James M. and Campbell, Roald F. (1968)

Educational Administration as a Social Process: Theory, research, practice, New York: Harper and Row.

Gibb, Cecil A. (1954) 'Leadership', in Gardner Lindzey (ed.) *Handbook of Social Psychology 2,* Cambridge, Mass.: Addison Wesley.

Gregg, Russell T. (1957) 'The Administrative Process', in Roald F. Campbell and Russell T. Gregg (eds.) *Administrative Behaviour in Education,* New York: Harper and Row.

Griffiths, Daniel E., Hemphill, John *et al.* (1961) *Administrative Performance and Personality,* New York: Teachers' College, Columbia University.

Gross, Neal, Mason, Ward S. and McEachern, A.W. (1958) *Explorations in Role Analysis: Studies of the School Superintendency Role,* New York: Wiley.

Gross, Neal, and Herriott, Robert E. (1965) *Staff Leadership in Public Schools: a Sociological Inquiry,* New York: Wiley.

Gulick, Luther, and Urwick, L. (1966) 'POSDCORB', in M. Chester Nolte (ed.) op. cit., p. 223.

Halpin, Andrew W. (1966) *Theory and Research in Education,* New York: Collier-Macmillan.

Halpin, Andrew W. and Winer, B. James (1957) 'A Factorial Study of the Leader Behaviour Descriptions', in Ralph M. Stogdill and Alvin E. Coons (eds.) *Leader Behaviour: Its Description and Measurement,* The Ohio State University, Bureau of Business Research Monograph No. 88, Section III.

Herriott, Robert E. and St. John, Nancy Hoyt (1966) *Social Class and the Urban School,* New York: Wiley.

Hills, R.J. (1960) 'A New Concept of Staff Relations', in M. Chester Nolte (ed.) op. cit., p. 372.

Hoyle, Eric (1965) 'Organizational Analysis in the Field of Education', *Educational Research,* VII, 97.

Hughes, Meredydd G. (1967) 'Simulated Situations', *Trends in Education,* **7,** 34.

Katz, Robert L. (1955) 'Skills of an Effective Administrator', *Harvard Business Review,* **33,** 33–42.

Laulicht, Jerome (1955) 'Role Conflict, the Pattern Variable Theory, and Scalogram Analysis', *Social Forces,* **33,** 250.

Levinson, Daniel J. (1959) 'Role, Personality and Social Structure in the Organizational Setting', *Journal of Abnormal and Social Psychology,* **58,** 170.

Lieberman, Seymour (1956) 'The Effects of Changes in Roles on the Attitudes of Role Occupants', *Human Relations,* **9,** 385.

Linton, Ralph (1952) 'Concepts of Role and Status', in G.E. Swanson, Theodore M. Newcomb and Eugene L. Hartley (eds.) *Readings in Social Psychology,* revised edition, New York: Holt, Rinehart.

Lipham, J.M. (1960) *Personal Variables Related to Administrative Effectiveness,* unpublished doctoral dissertation, University of Chicago, quoted in W.W. Charters and N.L. Gage (eds.) op. cit., p. 313.

Lipham, J.M. (1964) 'Leadership and Administration', in Daniel E. Griffiths (ed.) op. cit., ch. VI.

Lonsdale, Richard C. (1964) 'Maintaining the Organization in Dynamic Equilibrium', in Daniel E. Griffiths (ed.) op. cit., ch. VII.

Merton, Robert K. (1957a) *Social Theory and Social Structure*, revised and enlarged edition, New York: The Free Press of Glencoe.

Merton, Robert K. (1957b) 'The Role-set: Problems in Sociological Theory', *British Journal of Sociology*, **8**.

Nolte, Chester M. (ed.) (1966) *An Introduction to School Administration: Selected Readings*, New York: Macmillan, p. 259.

Oeser, O.A. and Harary, Frank (1962) 'A Mathematical Model for Structural Role Theory: I', *Human Relations*, **15**, 89.

Parsons, Talcott (1951) *The Social System*, London: Tavistock Publications.

Parsons, Talcott (1954) 'The Incest Taboo in Relation to Social Structure and the Socialization of the Child', *British Journal of Sociology*, **5**, 101.

Parsons, Talcott (1956) 'A Sociological Approach to the Study of Organizations: I and II', *Administrative Science Quarterly*, **3**.

Sarbin, Theodore R. (1954) 'Role Theory', in Gardner Lindzey (ed.) *Handbook of Social Psychology: I*, Cambridge, Mass.: Addison-Wesley.

Seeman, Melvin (1953) 'Role Conflict and Ambivalence in Leadership', *American Sociological Review*, **18**, 373.

Seeman, Melvin (1960) *Social Status and Leadership: the Case of the School Executive*, The Ohio State University, Bureau of Educational Research, Monograph No. 35.

Southall, Aidan (1959) 'An Operational Theory of Roles', *Human Relations*, **12**, 17.

Stogdill, Ralph M. (1948) 'Personal Factors associated with Leadership: a Survey of the Literature', *Journal of Psychology*, **25**.

Stogdill, Ralph M. and Shartle, C.L. (1955) *Methods in the Study of Administrative Leadership*, The Ohio State University, Bureau of Business Research, Monograph No. 80.

Stogdill, Ralph M., Scott Ellis L. and Jaynes, William E. (1956) *Leadership and Role Expectations*, The Ohio State University, Bureau of Business Research, Monograph No. 86.

Turner, Ralph H. (1962) 'Role-taking: Process vs. Conformity', in Arnold M. Rose (ed.) *Human Behaviour and Social Processes*, London: Routledge and Kegan Paul.

Westwood, L.J. (1966) 'Re-assessing the Role of the Head', *Education for Teaching*, **71**, 65.

Wilson, B.R. (1962) 'The Teacher's Role: a Sociological Analysis', *British Journal of Sociology*, **13**.

Applications

Chapter 6

Issues and Problems in Training the School Administrator

William Taylor

For an Englishman with an interest in educational administration an examination of the shelves in an American university library devoted to this field of study is initially a rather alarming experience. There are hundreds and hundreds of titles, only a minority of which are concerned with the familiar topics of meals and milk, finance and control and buildings and supplies. Instead millions of words are to be found on the role of the superintendent, the role of the principal, the role of the school board member; on supervision, evaluation, delegation, communication, professionalisation, certification and a dozen other processes. There are paradigms and models, theoretical constructs and conceptual taxonomies, analytical schema, dichotomous, bi-polar, ideal typical continuums and factorially structured four-celled frameworks. The effort required to read even a representative selection of the books and articles available is considerable, and apt to seem not particularly rewarding. For one thing, there is an enormous amount of repetition; the numerous introductions, basic texts and collections of readings seem to lean on many of the same sources and conceptual frameworks. Secondly, the prevailing tone of a good deal of the writing is prescriptive and inspirational. Genuflections in the direction of democracy, tolerance, group co-operation, community service and so on abound, and if the lists of qualities that are put forward as characteristic of the good administrator were ever to be rigorously applied as criteria for continued employment, it seems doubtful if there would be anyone left in office. Third, and no doubt in reaction to the programmatic confidence of some of these books, there is an increasing number of empirical investigations of aspects of the administrative process. Much of this work is methodologically impeccable. The research design is lean and functional, the instruments employed have been subjected to rigorous testing and evaluation, the analysis of data carried out with commendable precision on the ubiquitous high-speed computer. Sadly, however, the results of much of this effort, duly packaged within a supporting review of the literature, appropriate annotation, and a suitably restrained section of conclusions and recommendations for further work, all too frequently stimulate nothing except a series of questions regarding the worth of the whole exercise. It has been unkindly alleged that in this kind of academic game success is reckoned not by impact upon practice, but according to the number of references to one's work that appear as footnotes in other people's studies.

But it is easy to be critical about all this activity and publication, the very weaknesses of which are in part due to a willingness to face up to the problems that we in this country have only recently begun to recognise as important. The abundance of texts and books of readings may owe something to the premium placed upon publication in the American university, but it also reflects a demand generated by the extensive provision of courses in educational administration for potential and serving principals, deputy-principals, administrative assistants, supervisors, superintendents and all the other role-incumbents who are lumped together as the 'administration'. The stress upon positive advice, on the communication of human relations skills, on management technique in the widest sense, is a reflection of the practical and vocational nature of many of these courses, of the feeling that the purpose of teaching administration is to change administrative behaviour, to get better schools and better results. The recent shift towards a combination of empirical investigation and theory-building is a recognition of the inadequacies of much of the teaching that characterises such courses, and of the difficulty of laying down what administrators *should* do before we have a proper knowledge of what it is they do now, and why they act in one way rather than another.

To begin to study any social process, to examine and question the assumptions on which it is based, to expose the extent to which it is incongruent with the wider aims that we set ourselves, is at once to encourage innovation and change. In the absence of a single framework of traditions and values within which practices and procedures could be legitimised, the need for such study was felt earlier and more strongly in the United States than it has been in this country. But within the past twenty years we have begun to experience the kind of social and educational change that substantially increases the volume of educational decision-making required at every level, from that of the individual child, parent and teacher to that of the senior civil servant and the legislator. Whether it be the pupil's choice between dropping one subject rather than another, staying on rather than leaving, or the chief education officer's choice of presenting his committee with a plan based upon sixth-form colleges or of an all-through comprehensive school, the number of points at which some kind of choice between alternative possibilities must be exercised has increased enormously in recent years, as has the personal and social importance of the choices made. The unarticulated and dimly felt educational wants of parents and the public have begun to be converted into specific educational demands (Easton, 1965). On the part of teachers, heads, local administrators and civil servants there is growing recognition of the effects of the forms of educational organisation that we adopt in individual classrooms and in whole systems on levels of individual educability, aspiration and performance, and on the distribution of life chances. With this there has grown up a new interest in acquiring the kinds of knowledge and technique that will enable contemporary educational objectives to be operationalised, innovation managed, political pressures mediated and controlled and structural conflicts reconciled.

There is a danger that, in the face of this interest and demand for help, we may concentrate resources too narrowly on the provision of 'how to do it' courses, with a stress on technical competency rather than broader kinds of understanding and social skill. There is a growing number of week-end, one-week and part-time courses in school and system administration becoming available; the Department of Education and Science, many of the universities, the Tavistock Institute of Human relations, the College of Preceptors, local education authorities and teachers' organisations are all active in providing courses, conferences and workshop meetings for heads, senior teachers and educational administrators. The Nuffield Foundation, the Department of Education and Science and other funding bodies have provided support for the production of case and simulation materials for use in connection with these courses, and a variety of experiments are being tried in the use of closed circuit television, role-playing, curriculum and time-table analysis and other teaching devices. All this work is obviously worthwhile and important, but it needs to be underpinned by extensive programmes of more fundamental research and enquiry if it is to be really fruitful in promoting desired educational change. In this respect there is much that we can learn from the American experience; research, theory-building, and the education and training of practitioners need to be intimately associated with one another. Any sharp physical or temporal separation of these elements merely widens the gap between theory and practice that has already vitiated a good deal of work in wider fields of teacher education, and produces the kind of weaknesses that have already been referred to in this chapter. As a general principle, it is reasonable to argue that the study of educational administration and the teaching of educational administrators need to be undertaken in the same places by the same people. Some have argued that there is no place in the university for the kinds of course that provide skills and tools of the trade. These must be learned on the job, by means of specialised courses provided by employing bodies.

These skills are acquired through on the job experience...These are vocational skills. They do not challenge the intellect, they do not broaden one's scope of vision, they do not lend themselves to broad theory, they cannot be generalised to other areas. Most important, they cannot be adequately taught in a classroom situation (Liebman, 1953).

It seems unnecessary to adopt a dogmatic position on this issue. If the experience of other areas of study and teaching in the field of education is any guide, it is likely that non-university bodies will, in fact, come to provide most of the short courses and workshops, whilst universities will establish programmes of study for higher degrees and diplomas that place a greater stress upon general principles and theoretical analysis. In time, we may expect that most of the people responsible for short course and in-service teaching will themselves have experienced some relevant study at university level, and that the practical character of their offerings will be tempered by an awareness of on-going work on a broader front. But at the moment this is not the case. Whilst many of those responsible for existing courses for practitioners have had first hand experience of administration in schools and elsewhere, relatively few would claim any background in the disciplines that underlie educational study, or up-to-date knowledge of the literature of management and administration. Where specialists in these latter fields are brought in to help they, in their turn, often lack any real understanding of how the managerial imperatives of schools and colleges differ from those of industrial and commercial enterprises. Unless there is a fairly rapid expansion in the opportunities for research and the study of educational administration at university level, then this situation is likely to get worse; any increase in the range of short-course provision will merely exacerbate the existing problem.

II

Anyone who concerns himself with the study and teaching of educational administration, at whatever level, does so in the light of certain preconceptions about the nature of the administrative process and the goals of particular educational institutions. I want to define administration and management as functions that arise from the interpersonal and intergroup processes involved in system maintenance, task direction and goal attainment within the organisation, and from the relationship of the organisation to its publics and to other organisations. The significance of this stress upon function is to emphasise that administration and management are not autonomous activities; simply to teach educational administrators, heads and senior teachers about administrative practices and procedures, without giving a great deal of attention to the nature and goals of the organisation that has to be administered, is a fairly useless activity. Whilst the claim that there are a great number of administrative skills and processes that apply to all kinds of organisational settings is obviously true, and has undoubtedly done a great deal to support the growth of administrative studies, it can also get in the way of thinking clearly about the special kinds of expertise that the head of department, the head, the principal and the chief education officer need to do their jobs properly. In an important book, Walton defines administration in the following terms

Administration is (i) the carrying out of policies that have been deter-mined and accepted (ii) the direction of efforts of people working together in their reciprocal relations so that the ends of the organisation may be accomplished (iii) the maintenance of organisation. Fayol's analysis of the administrative process into the five functions of planning, organising, commanding, co-ordinating and controlling, and Gulick's restatement of these functions as planning, organising, staffing, directing, co-ordinating, reporting and budgeting, are attempts to break down the administrative activity into its component parts (Walton, 1959).

This is a very 'tight' definition of administration, and not one that can meaningfully be applied to the role of most of those who administer education at school or system level in this country. The head of a school not only administers but also makes policy—sometimes with only a minimum of consultation with those most likely to be affected. Although the position of the chief education officer varies widely from authority to authority, there are few that do not have some hand in the determination of the policy that the education committee adopts. At a national level, there is every indication that civil servants play a very important part in the shaping of educational policy. As Easton has indicated

A policy...consists of a web of decisions and actions that allocates values...Arriving at a decision is the formal phase of establishing a policy; it is not the whole policy in relation to a particular problem. A legislature can decide to punish monopolists; that is the intention. But an administrator can destroy or reformulate the decision by failing either to discover offenders or to prosecute them vigorously. The failure is as much a part of the policy with regard to monopoly as the formal law...If the law directs that all prices shall be subject to a specified form of control but black markets take root and the appropriate officials and the society as a whole accept their existence, the actual policy is not one of price control alone...(Easton, 1965).

Classical organisation theory, with its stress upon the kinds of activity that are referred to in the passage from Walton quoted above, also suffers from being too management-centred. Subramaniam has recently suggested that teaching along these lines '...offers to the manager a "myth", which enthuses and envigorates him and simultaneously trains him to offer to the managed this myth as the first draft of a contract, negotiable in parts and at the margins. He is given a sense of purpose by the myth but also prepared to some extent to face reality. He is psychologically armed much in the same way as the entrepreneur was (according to Max Weber) by the Protestant ethic...' (Subramaniam, 1967). In contrast, the approach to administrative preparation and professional development suggested here requires greater attention to be given to the total system of positions, relationships and goals within which the administrative function is exercised. There is less stress on acquiring knowledge or skill in administrative practices and procedures, more on the understanding of how educational objectives are defined and the means whereby resources may be organised to achieve them.

But perhaps a more serious objection to a definition of the kind suggested by Walton is that it invests the administrative process with a measure of autonomy that may be seen as interposing between an organisation and the achievement of its goals. Walton suggests, in fact, that the '...nature of the administrative process which is demanded by organisation is antithetical to the intrinsic functions of some organisations. In educational institutions this incompatibility is greater than it is in industry and less than it is in research institutions and in schools devoted exclusively to the creative arts, for example. However, since all organisations depend upon administration for their survival and maintenance, the solution to the problem inevitably involves some compromise between administrative necessity and educational activity' (Walton, 1965). But this seems to equate administration with bureaucratisation; there is indeed plenty of evidence to the effect that certain organisations, such as the research institutions to which Walton refers, are unproductive when highly bureaucratised, and there exist several case studies of how debureaucratisation has been accomplished (Whyte,

8

1967). Providing that we do not define administration too narrowly, we can still study how a relatively unbureaucratised institution such as a school or a college is administered, and try to provide some of the skills and knowledge that are involved in this process, without having to assume any conflict between administrative necessity and intrinsic goals. The definition suggested at the beginning of this section, with its emphasis upon administration as a function of internal and external organisational interaction, seems to provide the broader perspective that is required to accommodate the activities of educational administrators.

III

If the preceding definition of administration is accepted, it follows that the school administrator needs much more by way of preparation and opportunities for in-service development than can be afforded by courses in how to construct a timetable, order and maintain stock and equipment, and apply local authority and national rulings. If the head is, in fact, concerned with the identification of goals and objectives, the initiation of policy, the allocation of resources, the maintenance of positive human relations both within the school and between the school and the community, and with the professional growth of his colleagues, then he will need the kinds of knowledge and understanding that are rooted in a sub-culture, rather than derived from a set of readily communicable principles and rules. In the past, school administrators were members of a number of separate sub-cultures, each characterised by a good deal of social and educational homogeneity. Elementary school heads, for example, were distinctively different in social origin, schooling, further education, and experience from the heads of Grammar and Public Schools, local authority officials, and the senior civil servants responsible for education. In some cases there was very little overlap between such groups in respect of background and few opportunities for movement between them. Whatever the personality and other differences of the individuals who made up each group, they tended to share a common language and mode of speech, many common educational and social assumptions, and a common career structure. Within recent years, the boundaries of these sub-cultures have tended to become blurred by the expansion of educational opportunity, geographical and social mobility and the dissolution of some of the economic and ideological supports for the more obvious forms of hierarchy in educational organisation. Something of the former separation remains, especially in the structure of professional associations, but many of the differences are today more symbolic than real and there is a good deal of overlap between the groups.

It is much easier for persons to communicate and to work together, and there is much less to be learned, when they come from the same kinds of social background and have roughly comparable educational experiences than when they differ from each other in these respects. Within culturally homogeneous groups there is no need to spell everything out in words and written agreements, in rules and procedures, to find verbal forms by means of which to communicate experience, to define and control lines of communication (Steen, 1961). There is an existing basis for relationship and for action, and at best, a coherent and internally consistent traditional infrastructure of values and shared assumptions which facilitates and legitimises decision making. A concern with the inadequacies of a society that is without a well-defined pattern of unitary sub-cultures has permeated the writings of conservative educational and social critics during recent decades. In his *Notes towards the Definition of Culture* Eliot wrote of the way in which social groups that shared no common origins would meet together like committees (Eliot, 1948). Oakeshott has placed stress upon the way in which education serves to induct the individual into a culture, a language of discourse, an '...inheritance of feelings, emotions, images, visions, thoughts, beliefs, ideas, understandings, intellectual and practical enterprises, languages, relationships, organisations, canons and maxims of conduct, procedures, rituals, skills, works of art, books, musical compositions, tools, artifacts and utensils...' (Oakeshott, 1967). The all-important values and non-informational content of this culture cannot effectively be communicated by explicit teaching—'...the intellectual virtues may be imparted only by a teacher who really cares about them for their own sake and never stoops to the priggishness of mentioning them. Not the cry but the rising of the wild duck impels the flock to follow him in flight' (Oakeshott, ibid.).

It is possible that we have tended to place too much emphasis upon family background, early experience and the kind of school attended for the development of adult values and modes of conduct. Brim and Wheeler have recently drawn attention to the importance of *adult* socialisation.

The guiding assumption is simply that in many situations individuals remain highly adaptable and flexible, prepared to fit their behaviour to the demands of the current social context. The result is that we must not only look at underlying motives, that is, at how people have internalised deeply rooted features of the social order. Much can be learned about the processes of socialisation by taking a close look at the structures and situations within which it occurs (Brim and Wheeler, 1966).

As sociologists of science have emphasised, the scientist can only communicate with his fellows on the basis of a large number of shared assumptions and a considerable knowledge of the language and literature of his field, most of which is necessarily acquired as part of formal and informal educative processes within institutional settings (Storer, 1964). Social psychologists have also analysed the means by which the individual learns what may be called 'fluent social behaviour' in unfamiliar settings, and such behaviour would seem to have a good deal in common with the kinds of interaction that are implied by Oakeshott (Argyle, 1967; Goffman, 1961, 1963, 1965).

Adult socialisation clearly requires both education and training. The strength of the various sub-cultural traditions to which reference has been made has hitherto inhibited the necessity for much formal educational effort in educational administration and school management—or indeed in administration and management in general. Considerable effort is now being made in the field of business and commercial management training, but it seems doubtful if the general educational level of some of the students is adequate to support the kinds of practical and theoretical training that it is desired to provide. The Education Tables of the 1961 Census, published in 1966, show that only 11.8 per cent of the men and 25.6 per cent of the women classified as employers and managers of large establishments in England and Wales had terminal education ages of twenty or above, compared with 64.1 per cent of the men and 70.1 per cent of the women classified as self-employed professionals. At the other end of the scale, 70.0 per cent of the male employers and managers of large establishments, and 54.7 per cent of the women had not received any full-time education beyond the age of sixteen (General Register Office, 1961). Although differences in classification make direct comparisons difficult, there are indications that a far larger percentage of American managers have completed high school and experienced some years of college education—in 1960, 68.0 per cent of those in the United States classified as 'managers, officials and proprietors' were at least high school graduates and 35.4 per cent had had at least one year of college. The figures for the 'clerical, sales and kindred' classification were of the same order—65.6 per cent high school graduates and 28.0 per cent with at least a year of college education. In educational administration itself, the professionalisation of the principalship and superintendency that has been going on in recent years now demands that in many areas candidates for these positions will have completed a minimum number of hours of graduate work, and a Ph.D. or Ed.D. is frequently demanded of aspirants for senior posts.

Whether such specific requirements are reflected in improved operational performance is still an open question. In an ambitious study carried out in the United States, Gross and Herriott (1965) examined the correlates of a dimension of principal performance that they called 'Executive Professional Leadership' and defined as 'the efforts of an executive of a professionally staffed organisation to conform to a definition of his role that stresses his obligation to improve the quality of staff performance'. Executive Professional Leadership was found to be positively associated with pupil performance, teachers' morale and teacher performance. The education and experience of principals was then compared to see what kinds of course might be linked with E.P.L. Correlations with undergraduate and graduate courses in Education, and courses in educational administration were all negative—'the less extensive formal training of principals, the greater their E.P.L....It appears that previous administrative experience in public education has no apparent relationship to professional leadership'.

In the light of this and the earlier points that have been made about educational administration as a sub-culture, it is significant that there has been a move on the part of some universities in the United States to include a larger proportion of study in the humanities in the preparation and in-service education of school administrators (Blocker, 1967; U.C.E.A., 1967). Such an interest in the humanities may reflect the problem of giving the administrator skills in the delineation of goals. The whole concept of 'educational goals' is a vexed one. When we can assume a common administrative sub-culture, and when external constraints are relatively stable, goal definition presents few problems; the political or social conservative can manage without a philosophy or explicit ideology, but the radical must of necessity be intellectually self-conscious and attentive to aims. The very concept of goal has been subjected to attack both by organisation theorists and contemporary philosophers. Simon (1964), for example, states that 'it is doubtful if decisions are generally directed towards achieving *a* goal. It is easier, and clearer, to view decisions as being concerned with discovering courses of action that satisfy a whole set of constraints. It is this set, and not any one of its members, that is most commonly viewed as the goal of the action.' But later he suggests that in view 'of the hierarchical structure that is typical of most formal organisations, it is a reasonable use of language to employ organisational goal to refer particularly to the constraint sets and criteria of search that define roles at the upper levels'. Analyses of the decision-making process have in a number of studies provided evidence for the way in which goals and objectives shift in response to the particular kinds of feedback that are available within organisational settings (Bauer, 1967; Broadbent, 1967).

Another reason for an interest in humanistic content in courses for educational administrators may be the heuristic inadequacy of the concepts and theories of the field of educational administration itself. As Horvat (1965) has noted,

...In formal scientific endeavours a concept's usefulness is judged by the economy and power of the theoretical principles made possible by its use. According to such criteria, 'socio-economic class' is very useful (i.e. there are many propositions like the following: if x socio-economic class then y attitude toward progressive education) and the concept 'educational statesman' relatively useless (i.e. there are no attempts to use it in theoretical propositions)...

Educational administration as a field of study has generated few really powerful concepts of its own, although a number from the field of general administrative study, such as decision making, have provided theoretical focus. Most of the concepts used in the study of educational administration at the present time are derived from political science, law, social psychology and, to a lesser extent, philosophy. Most of those teaching educational administration are educators and administrators first, sociologists, psychologists and so forth secondarily and by adoption. This has two kinds of effect. First, because too few of those working in the field have had a fundamental training in one or more of the basic disciplines they are unable to apply sufficiently rigorous standards of scholarly relevance to their borrowings and derivations. Second, and perhaps more serious, educational administration has so far failed to make very much contribution to the disciplines from which it draws most of its concepts. As Gouldner (1965) has pointed out, there are a number of major concepts in sociology that emerged from applied studies, and which have now come to occupy an important place in the language of the subject. The contributions of the well-known Western Electric 'Hawthorne' study are illustrative in this respect. The possibility of a contribution of this kind is dependent upon the production of case-material, organised within a coherent conceptual structure. Unfortunately, however, the past few years have seen relatively few cases of this kind produced in the field of educational administration. The considerable number of teaching cases that have appeared, useful as they are, do not serve the same purpose. The stress upon theory building in a good deal of work in educational administration in the United States seems in many ways to have been premature; at the present we simply do not have enough information about how heads and principals operate, about how decisions at systems and national level are taken, to be able to develop an appropriate language and theoretical structure. Both for the sake of educational administration itself and for the disciplines on which it draws we would do well to concentrate our resources on description and middle-range analysis and, when we come to theory, to bear very much in mind the maxim *entia non sunt multiplicanda*. The existing limitations of knowledge in educational administration must necessarily limit the educational value of courses in the subject— the extent to which they can provide the individual with a viable and fruitful way of looking at his task, a groundwork of concepts and ideas that will enable theory and practice to interpenetrate one another and to bring about that subjective transformation of experience that is at the heart of all teaching endeavours. It may be a sense of these limitations that have helped to interest some professors of the subject in the part that the humanities might play in the education of the administrator.

A third reason for their interest might be that the humanities are seen as constituting a more potent means of adult socialisation than the behavioural sciences. And with this the argument of this section comes full circle. What the teacher of educational administration is looking for in the humanities is the basis for some kind of sub-cultural identity, some framework of shared values in terms of which heads and chief education officers and others in the education service can communicate with one another, some kind of common experience and symbol system that facilitates understanding and lubricates and humanises the operation of the rational econo-legal processes of bureaucratic decision-making. In part at least, the professionalisation of administration, the provision of formal courses of training and in-service education, represents an attempt to put back what social change, pluralism and more open access to administrative positions have taken away.

IV

To think of education and training in terms of existing roles is a concession to reality that fails to take full account of the implications of a functional definition of administration. These implications should properly include a willingness to examine administrative roles *de novo*, in terms of the kind of tasks that are generated by the internal and external relationships of an organisation pursuing a shifting pattern of objectives, rather than in accordance with any existing pattern of executive responsibility. It may be, for example, that the school of the future does not need a head of the traditional kind, or that his actions should be subject to the approval of his staff. Such a change has indeed come about in the role of the college of education principal, which has come more to resemble that of a university vice-chancellor than an autonomous head (Taylor, 1964, 1968). The idea has also been mooted that heads should be elected by the teachers and should hold office for only a limited period of years (Stone, 1963; Dixon, 1966).

Whilst it seems unlikely that ideas as radical as these will find ready acceptance for some time to come, those responsible for providing courses for heads and senior staff need to be very much aware of the kinds of change that are influencing the work of schools and the effects that these will have on the role of the school administrator.

Such awareness is facilitated by thinking of the provision of education and training for headship in terms of two key dimensions—*task* and *career*. There are two questions we need to ask about the first of these. What do heads do? Given the legitimacy and operationality of particular educational goals, what *should* they do in order to achieve these? (Taylor, 1968). It is the gap, if any, between the answers to these two questions that defines the area within which the training effort needs to be applied.

The second key dimension is that of *career*. What kind of education and experience have preceded appointment to a headship or administrative position? What factors are instrumental in the selection of people for such roles? What kinds of effect will training and subsequent experience have upon capability, performance and occupational movement? Each of these questions requires some kind of answer before we can hope to produce a satisfactory programme of preparation and in-service development for heads and administrators. All the programmes so far devised *imply* answers to these questions, but they are answers based upon subjective experience, hunch and guesswork, rather than upon a knowledge of facts which at the present time are simply not available.

The kinds of facts that are likely to be useful in furnishing better answers may emerge more clearly if we look at the questions in more detail. The first relates to heads' actual behaviour—the way in which they spend their time, the jobs that they do, the people with whom they interact. At the time of writing a study of such behaviour is being planned that will make use of diary entries, completed on a time sampling basis by a panel of volunteer heads in schools of different sizes and types. In order to collect and to handle information of this kind, a taxonomy has to be developed within which individual acts can be ordered and classified. By studying the frequency of each kind of behaviour included in the taxonomy, and by relating this to *school* variables, such as size, socio-economic environment and pattern of internal organisation, and *individual* variables, such as age, qualifications and experience, it should be possible to define the task of the head in behavioural terms. It can be hypothesised that such a definition will differ in important respects from existing interpretative accounts of what is involved in headship. In the field of business education, for example, a great deal of attention is given to the decision-making activity of the executive, yet behavioural studies of executives suggest that this may not be nearly so important an aspect of their work as is usually assumed. Reviewing such studies, Dubin (1962) states

The most outstanding (if not startling) facts presented by [these figures] is the small proportion of time spent on making decisions. If these studies are at all representative of what executives do, it would seem that making decisions, which is often considered their cardinal function, occupies a remarkably small share of their total working time.

It is also likely that the public image of headship gives too much credit for long term planning, and not enough for the difficulties of coping with the administrative and interpersonal minutiae of the daily round. Again, there are indicative studies from the world of business. March (1964) reports an experiment at the Carnegie Institute of Technology, in which executives were given a series of tasks involving routine communication, intermediate planning and long-term planning.

First, despite instructions to spend only one third of the time on routine matters, the subjects spent a good deal more than that even when the work load was relatively light. Second, consistently as the work load increased, subjects spent a smaller proportion of their time on planning activities. At peak loads, virtually no planning was evident.[1]

Having found out something about what heads do, we have to try to relate this behaviour to educational outcomes, to suggest links between particular actions and the 'results' that staff and pupils achieve. This is a matter of notorious difficulty; the very word 'results' makes educational hackles rise. The pernicious influence of 'payment by results' in the nineteenth century has been amply documented, as have the effects of the 'cult of efficiency' that for several decades pervaded American educational efforts (Callahan, 1963). The school is an organisation with diffuse output criteria. Educationalists cannot invoke apparently straightforward outcomes, such as profitability and volume of trade, to legitimise their activities. Even in the industrial and business field the merits of such criteria have been seriously questioned in recent years (Simon, 1964, 1965). Yet despite the difficulty of defining and evaluating results, it seems unnecessary to assume that such a task is impossible. Those parents who pay for their children's schooling, and those who are in a position to choose in which state school's catchment area they will live, are involved all the time in making decisions based upon some criteria of success. It would be naive to assume that such parents always define this solely in terms of examination results; a variety of other factors enter into parental, professional and public estimations of what constitutes a good school. We are beginning to document the way in which the school can

[1] This finding is reminiscent of the statement of a chairman of a large industrial concern, reported by Sampson (1962).
'What does a chairman's power amount to? "Ninety per cent of the time I'm just a superior nursemaid" said one of the chairmen. "I spend my time deciding to move Mr Smith to replace Mr Brown, trying to find another place for Mr Brown by persuading Mr Robinson that it's time for him to retire. The other ten per cent of the time is spent deciding about capital investment; and a lot of these decisions are forced on you by competition. That's what I was told when I took over—but I didn't believe it then. Most of your time is spent in the engine room. Only occasionally do you go up to the bridge; then you lash the helm and go down again"'.

exercise an independent influence on the educability, career assumptions and out of school life of its pupils, to recognise the kinds of facts to the importance of which parental behaviour and attitudes have long been testimony (Powers *et al.*, 1967).

There is a great need in education at the present time for studies that identify objectives, develop criteria by means of which the achievement of these may be tested, and relate the behaviour and activities of heads, teachers and others to the degree of success that schools achieve. By building up our store of information on these points we shall be in a much better position to specify what kinds of action and decisions are most likely, in given circumstances, to result in particular educational outcomes, and to know what kinds of investment of effort on the part of the head is likely to be most rewarding. Thus the second question linked to the task dimension of the head's role—what should the head do?—can only be answered by reference to educational values and objectives, and by finding out more about the way in which administrative action and educational outcomes are related to one another. On the basis of the information thus produced, we can more accurately determine the skills and knowledge that the head can best use, and try to build these into our programmes of preparation and in-service work.

The other key dimension that needs to be thought about in relation to preparatory and in-service work with heads is that of *career*. Here again there is a paucity of information. We know very little about the kinds of people who become heads, the ways in which they differ from their colleagues who remain in the classroom or who go elsewhere, the motives that impel them to apply for headships. We have some fascinating details of how some of the heads of the great public schools obtained their jobs and how they performed them, but precious little about the head of the state primary or secondary school today (Bamford, 1967; Annan, 1965).

Nearly all heads have considerable experience in the classroom and many have previously held posts of responsibility in charge of departments, or as deputy heads. The successful applicant for a headship is usually better academically qualified than most of his colleagues in the same type of school. It is becoming exceptional for a non-graduate head to be appointed to a secondary school, and a record of regular attendance at in-service courses strengthens the position of aspirants to headships in all types of schools. It is uncommon for a man or woman to be appointed to a headship with less than eight or ten years teaching experience; it is unusual for a person to be appointed to a first headship over the age of fifty. But these statements all represent statistical frequencies, not rules governing appointments. At present, any programme of study for heads and senior staff in schools has to be designed to take into account a very wide variety of previous educational level and experiences. Some of the participants will have no record of formal work in education, having entered teaching immediately after graduation with a 'subject' degree from university. Others may have a postgraduate certificate in education, an advanced diploma in one or more of the disciplines that underlie educational study, and a Master's degree obtained by research in education or high-level examined study in one of its aspects. Whilst it does not follow that a person's academic record is a certain index of his capacity to profit from work in the area of school administration, or that the best qualified have the best role-performance, this variety of background does indicate the difficulty of designing a course that builds on previous knowledge and applies it within the framework of administrative activity.

The fact that the better qualified candidate is more likely, other things being equal, to obtain a headship or senior position, means that there is some kind of link between, on the one hand, the efforts of the universities and other course and award providing bodies and, on the other, the process whereby heads are selected for appointment. But this link is tenuous and indirect. The dynamics of the selection process in this country are virtually unknown. We certainly do not know how much weight is attached to formal qualifications and course experience. The lay appointing committee is presumably looking for an individual with certain capabilities and potential, and with a good previous record. Since there is no formal evidence available regarding the association between particular kinds of experience and qualification and subsequent success, they presumably operate largely by personal impression and by hunch. All too often appointments are made without due cognisance being taken of the role demands of the post concerned. Burnham (1964) has suggested that the senior administrators in the school need to satisfy between them both *instrumental* and *expressive* functions, and it does seem that in many schools, as a consequence of personal disposition and role-adaptation, there is some measure of 'specialisation' in these respects on the part of the senior staff. When the head, the deputy, or other senior member retires or moves on, the nature of the gap that has to be filled is defined by a whole series of informal and semi-formal role expectations. Yet, unless means exist whereby this kind of information can be fed in to the selection process, the appointing committee is unlikely to be aware of the expectations that exist, and least of all when these should be respected and when they should be consciously denied. A head who is happier and more effective with people than with paperwork, and a deputy whose interests and skills are the opposite, may make a very effective team. But two of the same kind may be disastrous.

During the next few years we are likely to find ourselves taking some important decisions, either knowingly or by default, about the part that qualifications in educational administration should play in determining an individual's prospects of a headship. If we begin to provide some kind of preparatory training that is expressly directed towards headship, and appointing committees begin to favour candidates with such training, then the first important step has been taken towards professionalising school administration.

Although the discussion in this section has been concentrated upon the head, its central point is relevant to the provision of education and training for all kinds of administrative roles. Such preparatory and in-service work must be planned in relation to the tasks the administrator is likely to have to perform both immediately and in the future; it must be viewed within the total context of the individual's career and the means by which he is selected for an administrative position, taking into account levels of general and professional education, experience, and the way in which his orientation towards an administrative role has been fostered.[1]

---

[1] It would be of interest in this context to know how the future head or local authority education officer engages in what Merton (1957) calls 'anticipatory

V

This chapter has suggested some of the issues that are involved in answering, in relation to educational administration, the question 'Who teaches what to whom, when, where and how?' Included in the 'what' there is clearly a good deal of useful knowledge which the administrator might possess. A glance at any text-book of the subject, or the section headings of the National Union of Teachers handbook on school administration, indicates some of the ways in which this might be organised. But the acquisition of such knowledge is in many ways the least important aspect of courses of preparation and in-service education for school and system administrators. Of much greater importance is the development of certain cognitive and social skills, the learning of a variety of intellectual strategies. Duhl (1967) has stated the matter well in relation to the patient/therapist relationship.

When the patient comes to a therapist reporting a current crisis, he usually asks for help in reaching a certain goal. If the therapist were a planner, he would probably sit down and outline five steps for the patient to take. If, however, the therapist simply gives a patient five steps to follow, nothing will happen. He must first teach the patient the step-by-step process of assimilating new information, of reconceptualising the world, of looking towards generalised goals, and of thinking about how certain immediate steps may be directed towards these generalised goals.

What the study of educational administration provides for the administrator is not 'facts' but an understanding of the *kinds* of facts that are relevant to his task, where they may be obtained, and the use to which they may be put. To teach within this field is to offer the student new ways of structuring his perceptions within a familiar educational and social landscape. It is thus not so much the content of such teaching that deserves attention, but the principles in accordance with which it is organised and the methods by which it is carried on.

At the risk of over-simplification, four main ways of teaching

socialisation' towards his future role, and how far his orientation towards such roles is particularised or is part of a more general desire for promotion. A study of the recruitment of lecturers to colleges of education staff showed that many candidates for these positions were at the same time actively seeking headships and advisory positions with local authorities (Taylor, 1966).

educational administration can be singled out for comment. First, and most obviously, there are the standard techniques of lecture, seminar and discussion group, used in every university and in most of the courses provided by other bodies. The drawbacks of the lecture as a means of communicating information need not be discussed here; they have been given a good deal of consideration by groups and individuals concerned with university teaching methods in recent years (Hale report, 1965; Collier, 1968). Despite the weaknesses of the lecture method, its cheapness and organisational simplicity are likely to keep it in the centre of the teaching stage for some time to come. But lectures can be of positive usefulness in other directions, in illustrating a strategy, a way of approach to a problem, in exemplifying how someone with expert claims tackles a particular subject matter. The lecture can be one of the ways in which practitioners are introduced to both good and bad cognitive procedures, to the ways of thought that are characteristic of the disciplines associated with the study of administration. Seminars and discussion groups can also be used in this way, with the added advantage that there is more opportunity for the teacher to become aware of student's difficulties in understanding, and for students to participate actively in the learning process.

Active participation is also characteristic of the case and simulation techniques that form the second group of teaching methods (Watson and Taylor, 1969; Taylor, 1965 and 1969). But this is not the only justification for such techniques. In the study of education, as in so many other fields, the only answer to the programmatic, inspirational and hortatory generalisations that have characterised a good deal of educational discourse, has been a shift into empirical and analytical modes of enquiry. But too exclusive a devotion to the analytical carries the risk that the inter-relationships between factors that enter into educational actions and processes will be neglected. In seeking to alter one part of the system we may fail to take account of the need for corresponding changes elsewhere. For example, we might produce conclusive evidence regarding the favourable educational effects, under experimental conditions, of 'de-streaming' secondary schools. But if we try to implement these findings as an educational reform, without at the same time altering the other organisational features of the school and the attitudes and habits of teachers, such as a devotion to class-teaching, which have both supported and followed from stream-ing, then the reform is unlikely to succeed.[1] Systems analysts emphasise that information within and between organisms is not linear (cause and effect on two variable systems) but variable, reverberating, circular transactions establishing com-plicated chains of causation in which all effects become causes and vice versa (Grinker, 1967). When we select any particular feature of a system for study, we run the risk that everything else in the system becomes environment for the feature under investigation—Swift (1965) has drawn attention to some of the hazards that arise in conceptualising 'environment' when we examine social influences on educability and performance. Systems of social action are of such complexity that they cannot properly be understood by isolating particular acts for independ-ent analysis. Perception and social action are non-linear in respect of both space and time. Analyses of such perception and action find it difficult to cope with the problem of simultaneity: the human propensity to be responding and acting on a number of different levels at the same time, especially when face to face relationships are involved (MacKenzie, 1967; Goffman, 1959, 1961). The study of written and dramatised cases, the working of simulated exercises based on 'in-basket', film, or video-tape materials, can help to balance the rigorous analysis that is required in other respects of a course in educational administra-tion. Such methods have the great advantage that they permit control of the perceptual load and conceptual vocabulary with which the student has to deal, whilst at the same time retaining contact with the multi-layered, non-linear, perceptually dense reality of the world of decision and action.

A third group of methods can be classified under the heading of 'sensitivity training'. In broad terms, these seek to enhance the individual's awareness of the nuances of face to face and

[1] As Husen (1967) has commented in relation to educational technology: 'The introduction of new technologies, such as television, programmed material, correspondence courses and other audio-visual material, has to be conceived in relation to a thoroughly revised work organisation and its corollary of revised teacher training... the new devices are often included as mere extras hitched on to existing practices, with resulting lack of significant effect upon outcomes.'

small group interaction. In the United States such methods owe their origins to the activities of the National Training Laboratory (Bradford *et al.*, 1963), whilst in this country the Tavistock Institute of Human Relations has played a leading part in sponsoring courses and programmes of study (Rice, 1964). The chief technique of sensitivity training is the *Training Group*

A T group is a relatively unstructured group in which individuals participate as learners. The data for learning...are the transactions among members, their own behaviour in the group, as they struggle to create a productive and viable organisation, a miniature society; and as they work to stimulate and support one another's learning within that society...T group members must establish a process of enquiry in which data about their own behaviours are collected and analysed simultaneously with the experience that generates the behaviours...(Bradford *et al.*, 1963).

The opportunities for educational administrators to participate in full-scale T groups in this country have so far been very limited, but there are now a growing number of courses and workshop meetings that use related techniques and which recognise that 'the first organisational principle of in-service training is to get each person into a small, supportive group in which the members' responsibility is to help the others' (Thelan, 1956; see also Richardson, 1967 (i) and (ii)).

Finally, there are the teaching methods that combine university or other courses in educational administration with periods of practical work in schools, local education authority offices and elsewhere. In the United States there are a variety of field experience programmes in operation, one of the most interesting of which is the *internship* (Walker, 1968; Van Miller, 1965). The intern gains experience of administrative situations in schools, in consultancy and advisory work, and in the central office. During this time his work is supervised by an experienced senior administrator and by the staff of the university institution at which he is registered. Some internships carry credit towards degrees in administration. The existing career structure for administrative positions in education would not make it easy for such a programme to be introduced in this country, but there are a number of attempts being made to combine practice in and the academic study of administration by running evening and one-day-a-week seminars for heads, with a good deal of assigned work that has to be undertaken between meetings.[1]

A balanced programme of preparation and in-service development for the school and system administrator could well include some use of each of the approaches that have been outlined in the preceding paragraphs. Such teaching is likely to be much more productive of further intellectual growth and practical skill if the students concerned have some previous acquaintance with the framework of the study of education, and are aware of the contributions made to it by psychology, sociology, history and philosophy. Educational administration, conceived as a branch of the history of education, could reasonably be taught at a fairly elementary and descriptive level. But if the approach to educational administration proposed by this book is accepted, it follows that the subject requires a good deal of prior understanding of basic educational concepts and ideas if it is to make sense to the student and be of use to the practitioner.

Decisions about the allocation of educational resources have to take into account not only the importance of claims for attention, but also the extent to which there is likely to be a useful return for the effort made. The case for giving more attention to the education and training of educational administrators satisfies both these criteria; it is to be hoped that the developments that are discussed elsewhere in these pages will soon be reflected in the content and structure of a wider provision of relevant courses and programmes of study.

Bibliography

Annan, N. (1965) *Roxbrugh of Stowe*, London: Longmans.

Argyle, M. (1967) *The Psychology of Interpersonal Behaviour*, London: Penguin.

Bamford, T.W. (1967) *The Rise of the Public Schools*, London: Nelson.

Bauer, R. (1967) 'Societal Feedback', *Social Goals and Indicators for American Society, II*, The Annals of the American Academy of Political and Social Sciences, 373, September.

Blocker, C. E. (1966) 'Clinical and Humanistic Training as a Foundation for Effective Administration', *Journal of Educational Administration*, IV, 2.

Bradford, L.P., Gibb, J.R. and Benne, K.D. (1964) *T-Group Theory and Laboratory Method*, New York: Wiley.

[1] Part-time evening courses in school administration have been run for some years by the University of Oxford Institute of Education, and a one-day-a-week seminar for heads is being undertaken at Bristol during 1968 and 1969.

Brim, O. and Wheeler, S. (1966) *Socialisation after Childhood*, New York: Wiley.

Broadbent, D.E. (1967) 'Aspects of Human Decision Making', *Advancement of Science*, **24**, 119, September.

Burnham, P.S. (1968) 'The Deputy Head', in Allen, B. (ed.) *Headship for the Seventies*, Oxford: Blackwell.

Callahan, R.E. (1964) *Education and the Cult of Efficiency*, Chicago: University of Chicago Press.

Collier, K.G. (1968) *New Dimensions in Higher Education*, London: Longmans.

Dixon, R.G.D. (1966) 'Are Principals Obsolete?', in Nolte, M.C. *An Introduction to School Administration*, New York: Macmillan.

Dubin, R. (1962) 'Business Behaviour Behaviourally Viewed' in Strother, G.B. (ed.) *Social Science Approaches to Business Behaviour*, London: Tavistock Publications.

Duhl, L. J. (1967) Discussion contribution in *Daedalus*, Summer.

Easton, D. (1965) *A Systems Analysis of Political Life*, New York: Wiley.

Eliot, T. S. (1948) *Notes Toward the Definition of Culture*, London: Faber and Faber.

General Register Office, Census 1961, England and Wales, *Education Tables*, 1966.   [Doubleday.

Goffman, E. (1959) *The Presentation of Self in Everyday Life*, New York:

Goffman, E. (1961) *Encounters*, Indianapolis: Bobbs Merrill.

Goffman, E. (1963) *Asylums*, New York: Doubleday.

Gouldner, A.W. (1965) 'Explorations in Applied Social Science', in Gouldner, A.W. and Miller, S.M. (eds.) *Applied Sociology*, New York: The Free Press of Glencoe.

Grinker, R.R. (1967) Introduction to Grinker, R.R. (ed.) *Toward a Unified Theory of Human Behaviour*, New York: Basic Books.

Gross, N. and Herriott, R.E. (1965) *Staff Leadership in Public Schools*, New York: Wiley.   [London: H.M.S.O.

Hale Report (1964) *Report of the Committee on University Teaching Methods*,

Horvat J.J., Bridges, E.M. and Sroufe, G.E. (1965) *Case Studies in Educational Administration*, An information storage and retrieval system, Columbus, Ohio: University Council for Educational Administration.

Husen, T. (1967) 'Thoughts Concerning Educational Technology' *International Review of Education*, XIII, 1.

Liebman, C.S. (1953) 'Teaching Public Administration: Can we Teach What we don't Know?', *Public Administration*, XXIII, 3.

Mackenzie, W.J.M. (1967) *Politics and Social Science*, London: Penguin Books.

March, J.G. (1964) 'Business Decision Making', in Leavitt, H.J. and Pondy, L.R. (eds.) *Readings in Managerial Psychology*, Chicago: University of Chicago Press.

Oakeshott, M. (1967) 'Learning and Teaching' in Peters, R.S. (ed.) *The Concept of Education*, London: Routledge and Kegan Paul.

Powers, M.J. *et al.* (1967) 'Schools for Delinquency?' *New Society*, **10**, 264.

Revans, R.W. (1967) 'Quantitative Methods and Management Research' in Mossom T.M. (ed.) *Teaching the Process of Management*, London: Harrap.

Rice, K. (1964) *Learning for Leadership*, London: Tavistock Publications.

Richardson, J. E. (1967 (i)) *The Environment of Learning*, London: Nelson.

Richardson, J.E. (1967 (ii)) *Group Study for Teachers*, London: Routledge and Kegan Paul.

Sampson, A. (1964) *An Anatomy of Britain*, London: Longmans.

Simons, H.A. (1964) 'On the Concept of Administrative Goal', *Administrative Science Quarterly*, **9**, 1, June.

Simon, H.A. (1965) *The Shape of Automation*, New York: Harper and Row.

Simon, H. (1964) 'On the Concept of Organisational Goal', *Administrative Science Quarterly*, **9**, 1.

Steen, H. (1966) 'The British Administrator's World', Review of Willson, F.M.G. *Administrators in Action*, Toronto: University of Toronto Press 1961, in Hawley, C.E. and Weintraub, R.G. *Administrative Questions and Political Answers*, Princeton: Van Nostrand.

Stone, E. (1963) 'The Role of the Headteacher in English Education', *Forum*, **6**, 1, Autumn.

Storer, N.W. (1966) *The Social System of Science*, New York: Holt, Rinehart.

Subramaniam, V. (1966) 'The Classical Organisation Theory and its Critics', *Public Administration*, **44**, Winter.

Swift, D.F. (1965) 'Educational Psychology, Sociology and Environment: A Controversy at Cross-purposes', *British Journal of Sociology*, **16**.

Taylor, W. (1964) 'The Training College Principal', *Sociological Review*, **12**, 2.

Taylor, W. (1965) 'The Use of Simulations in the Training of Educational Administrators in England', *Journal of Educational Administration*, **III**, 1.

Taylor, W. (1966) *The Staff of the Colleges of Education*, Oxford: University of Oxford Department of Education (mimeographed).

Taylor, W. (1968) 'Training the Head', in Allen, B. (ed.) *Headship for the Seventies*, Oxford: Blackwell.

Taylor, W. (1969) 'Cases, Simulations and Games: An Overview', in Taylor, W. and Watson, L.E. (eds.) *Cases and Simulations in the Teaching of Educational Administration* (forthcoming).

Thelan, H.A. (1954) *Dynamics of Groups at Work*, Chicago: University of Chicago Press.

University Council for Educational Administration (1967) *Annual Report* 1966/67, Columbus, Ohio: The Council.

van Miller (1965) *The Public Administration of American School Systems*, New York: Collier-Macmillan.

Walker, W.G. (1969) 'Trends and Issues in the Preparation of Educational Administrators', in Baron, G., Cooper, D., and Walker, W.G. (eds.) *Educational Administration: International Perspectives*, Chicago: Rand McNally.

Walton, J. (1959) *Administration and Policy Making in Education*, Baltimore: The Johns Hopkins Press.

Watson, L.E. and Taylor, W. (1969) 'In-basket Simulations and the Training of Educational Administrators', in Taylor, W. and Watson, L.E. (eds.) op. cit.

Whyte, W.F. (1967) 'Models for Building and Changing Organisations' *Human Organisations*, **26**, 1/2.

Chapter 7
Administration and Curriculum Change
J. G. Owen

No single and outstanding model for the administration of change in the fabric of teaching exists in Britain. Discrete, unrecorded experiences there must be in plenty, but an attempt to provide any empirical model suffers from this very discreteness. This chapter, while not intended to be over-nakedly empirical, is an attempt to show the critical moments in the sequence of activities through which the administrator has to work in the process of change. Fact and theory are at this stage intermingled, for systematic change of curriculum is still too young for there to be adequate data upon which to base any one style of description. At this stage, too, those values which are involved in curriculum revision are insufficiently explicit to reveal their subtleties and ambiguities.

A conception of change aimed at the improvement of a child's learning experience has many nuances of judgment which lie behind visible activity. New work in the humanities, for instance, can aim at increasing the pupil's confidence in the rational process by which he reaches moral decisions or at giving him a greater stability and sensitivity in his reliance on feelings. It can seek to heighten his individualism or to make him more wholly a member of a society which he understands. Or even, in more easily definable parts of the curriculum, change in, for instance, mathematics and science can outwardly follow similar lines in improving knowledge, heightening a pupil's confidence in dealing with concepts and in relating the subject to the world in which he will work after leaving school—but there can be differing (and perhaps contradictory) implications in the emphasis which is placed on the social relevance of these subjects. And corresponding to the differences of aim and of implication in the content of the changing curricula there are differences in the strategies of change and in the strategies of co-operation between those who can bring it about. Within the area of partnership, as well as within the justification of change itself, there lie concepts of value which still have to be argued out. Is it the teacher, the encouragement to think anew, and the provision of retraining which must come first? Or is it the pupil whose needs must be re-defined? Or is it a changing society which must urgently and freshly be described so that we may know the specific modifications which are required of what is taught at school? The judgment of where first to place the weight of effort is a decision about values. These values are seldom made explicit and this chapter has to accept that limitation. But in an early statement of the role of administration in the process of curriculum change in Britain, to leave implicit what cannot otherwise be teased out may not be entirely frustrating. It may encourage other, more rigorous, contributions to the study.

I

Who are the administrators who are concerned with curriculum change? They are all those who initiate, design, disseminate, finance and facilitate reform. They are found in specialist bodies such as The Schools Council, in the secretariats of teachers' associations, among the senior administrative staff of local authority associations, in the Department of Education and Science, among directors (and their staffs) of Institutes of Education, among Her Majesty's Inspectorate, among principals of Colleges of Education and, particularly, among heads of schools and senior administrators in local education authorities. Apart from those who work with an exclusive interest (e.g. The Schools Council) the bulk of day-to-day decisions about curriculum change fall to those who work in local authorities. The definition of an administrator in this chapter is therefore purposely narrow—for in its local context it even excludes the heads of schools. The reason for this is that heads are still in practice talked about and thought of as teachers. They are expected to know about, and to be involved in, curriculum change. The local administrator, unlike those in the Department of Education and Science or in the secretariat of a local authority association or teachers' association, cannot avoid seeing very specific things happening (or failing to happen) to the teaching of particular groups of children in particular schools. But he is not generally expected to know much about curriculum. Once a teacher becomes an administrator he is expected by some to forgo any claims to competence in this field.

The demarcation between administration and education described in terms of the demarcation between administrator and teacher should now be largely meaningless. That it may still be thought to have a residual meaning causes confusion and diffidence. Four arguments ought to be enough to dispel this confusion and to show that the administrator has to be deeply involved in curriculum change if its effects are to be at all extensive or long-lasting.

First, since 1947 a succession of what have appeared as nothing more than problems of educational administration have changed gradually into a series of opportunities for improvement. Whether it has been the conception of secondary education for all, or the reorganisation of secondary schools, or school building programmes, or the idea of compensation through education, or the admission of a wider band of pupils to public examinations, the underlying aim of maximising social justice has demanded that administration should, among other things, be increasingly concerned with quality and with growth. This has helped to provide a changing setting for the answering of what are, in the end, the three single most important questions for the pupil—what is he to learn, how is he to learn it, and why should he learn it.

These three questions have to be answered in any movement towards the renewal of the curriculum: if the pace of that movement is quickening then administration cannot stand away. The 1944 Education Act delegates oversight of curriculum to local education authorities. This oversight is in turn delegated to the managers and governors of schools and, again, to the heads of schools. To diminish this oversight would be a threat to the ill-defined freedom of the teacher: but to pretend that that freedom in the larger matter of curriculum is very much more than a freedom to choose upon whom to be dependent is certainly fallacious and perhaps hypocritical. To avoid that hypocrisy and to ensure that what happens to the pupil, at his first contact with learning, can be reviewed and improved cannot too fancifully be claimed an important aspect of social justice. Local administration therefore has to be involved, but it has neither to threaten nor to condescend to those with whom it engages.

Secondly, the functions of an administrator are not usually expected to include the development of a particular philosophy of education. It has been accurate in the past to stress the full freedom of the head as regards the internal organisation, time-table, syllabuses and those other activities of his school which need to be based on some philosophy, or at least some plan, of education. We can explain these different expectations by refer-ence to a longer history of the purposes of universal schooling and to the evolution of a school system which was insulated against social pressures (Baron and Tropp, 1961). But more recent events have shown that neither the insulation nor the freedom of schools can continue to be thought of as sources of simple strength. Because neither a head nor a school can, in fact, operate in isolation, a choice of allies must be made. If positive co-operation with others is necessary for a school to get the most out of itself, there has to be a reliance less upon a tenuous and over-generalised connection such as has, for instance, for long existed between grammar schools and univer-sities than upon a connection with those activists, facilitators and interpreters, from any source within education, who are best able to give reality and practical effect to the schools' (limited) choice of how to educate their pupils. For the school to need to find allies heightens, if anything, the importance for the head and his colleagues to agree, both philosophically and practically, on their objectives. But the allies who can enable the school to re-think its work effectively need to share in that thinking; they need a philosophy of their own which is consonant with that of the schools. If the administrator is to be a chief ally he has to be able to meet the teacher on equal terms in his thinking about the purposes and methods of education.

In the exercise of the choice of how to educate, the organisa-tion of the school system, as well as the internal organisation of individual schools, has importance. Both have previously stressed the *distribution* as opposed to the *creation* of authority.

The present day school and its pupils will feel that it is less important simply to accept authority than to understand its purposes. To understand the purposes of curriculum (as being, in some ways, the most authoritative element in a school's activities) needs the recognition that curriculum itself has its own authority. Therefore, what is new in curriculum has to find a new authority: it will be a participant authority and not a transmitted one and the co-operation which leads to participation has to be fostered both within and outside the school. The administrator will be unable to help unless his own thinking can contribute to that authority.

As an example, a first necessity of change in the curriculum is to ask which pupils are being benefited and how: except in a system of highly individualised teaching (towards which we may be working) the fact that children are *taught* as a group (in the traditional manner of class-teaching rather than in participant group activity in drama, dance or community service) means that someone may suffer, because the pace is too fast or too slow, or the material too difficult or too easy. Any curriculum is open to objection (more perhaps from the parent than from the pupil) from those who do not benefit as much as the majority. No curriculum can be invulnerable (except the individualised one) but it must be as resistant to objection as possible.

New curriculum cannot afford to rely on an authoritarian justification; it has to make its own arguments clear, but with an authority at least equal to a curriculum which was previously required by, say, the 'eleven-plus' or by an external examination syllabus in a secondary school. And it will not do to modify and expand the structure of examinations and to hope, thus, to transmute what is new and well done in a few schools into requirements which should be met by all schools. For this could only be done if we thought that primary school children should once more be measured in their achievement by examination or if we could afford the social injustice suffered by those who will never pass an examination of any significance, or if we felt that we should altogether take away from the teacher the responsibility of meeting the particular needs of particular groups of pupils.

The authority must come from another source; it must in fact be created by teachers acting in liaison with the users of school education (whether employers, parents, further education, professional bodies or universities). Those who change the curriculum are increasingly accountable to these users and to a public which is becoming better informed about schooling. We can only be accountable if both the educators and the users of education understand and agree about what is being done in schools and about the degree to which this meets the users' needs. The school needs a synoptic view from the outside of what it is doing as well as its own view from the standpoint of the pupil. This duality of viewpoint, to which the administrator should contribute, protects new curriculum against distortion and misunderstanding.

Third, the administrator has to be aware of the differing circumstances and characteristics of change. Unless these are known, the attempt to assist and strengthen innovation in an orderly way will be frustrated: changes differ from one another in their points of origin, in the degree to which they need to be encouraged, in their mode and scale of implementation, in their chances of survival, in their diffusion beyond the first and individual attempt, and in the assessment and evaluation to which they are subjected. They differ, too, in the difficulties which surround the identifying of agents who can bring them into being and in the demand they make for leadership at each stage of their life. The genealogy is complex and has to be learned.

Fourth, and as a corollary to an awareness of the differing circumstances of change, there has to be an awareness of the difficulties which encompass the administrator himself. He is unlikely to help the process along unless he realises the real risks of resistance, conflict, fear and misunderstanding which surround the appraisal, let alone the acceptance, of innovation. While the dangers are reasonably well charted in the literature of curriculum renewal in other countries, there is in Britain at present little other than the administrator's own experience and insight upon which to base any hope of minimising these risks and of giving reassuring and confident leadership.

II

Guidelines, other than those drawn from unrelated experience, are few for the administrator who stands outside the school but who, nevertheless, has responsibility for assisting in a process which is a very intimate concern of the school. The quietist will talk of the freedom of the teacher and will let the push come from that direction. The administrator who, wanting to act the part of facilitator, is too facile will risk taking on too much and will be almost bound to complain of what he sees as poor co-operation; the moderate will find himself acting on inexplicable intuition, walking along a none too secure edge between too much interference and too little concern. The view of himself which the administrator favours in other, more traditional administrative tasks, will colour his view of what new form of activity is appropriate to change: the view will differ from man to man and each will be uncertain of his position. Although he will usually have gone through a somewhat similar stage of confusion about what is expected of him at least once earlier in his career, in his translation from class-teaching to an administrative post, he is unlikely to find the earlier experience helpful: to change from the school to an education office is to move between two externally, at least, stable styles of operation. But the comfort of stability is absent when changes begin which affect something other than the visible and generally comprehended parts of organisation and system. Fundamental questions of the quality of education have to be raised and in answering these no one starts off in a position of comfort: each participant, be he head, assistant teacher, administrator or adviser, is faced with questions which test him as an educator. The fact that he earns his money in education does not necessarily make him an educator.

While it would be over-simple to pretend that established roles bind administrators to precedent, or assistant teachers to somebody else's syllabus, or advisers/inspectors to some Platonic scheme for the assessment of teaching, it is neither pointless nor an over-simplification to stress that the equation of curriculum developer with educator calls for an ability to appraise, to create and to organise in a manner and on a scale which has not previously been necessary. Creation, appraisal and organisation are central to innovation; training in the role of innovator has not been provided for the teacher, and even less for the administrator. Moreover, to the extent that either has been explicitly trained, or has acquired skills in, the preservation of status quo, change produces conflict. When the conflict is internal to the person, it produces uncertainty; when it is external and happens between people, it is likely to produce resistance.

III

In terms of curriculum, whether or not this is defined as everything that happens to the pupil within, or in connection with, the school, the common sense of systematic change requires that it should be worked out in a partnership between every person who can make a contribution, from schools, from administration, from universities and from teacher associations. A cynic might say that it is not common sense but the state of politics in education in England which make this partnership a necessity. But, either way, partnership is necessary and in the process of organising it the administrative ally is almost bound to have more levers ready to his hand than others. It is he who has to act between the limits of diffidence and brashness. An awareness of these limits is essential.

While there must be few senior administrators who feel that they were appointed solely to control, as superordinates, that which happens in schools and elsewhere, there may be equally few who can connect the ill-defined authority of their position with their role in a new situation. In his relationship with a lay education committee the administrator finds himself in a variety of roles: adviser, employer's man, consultant, and, throughout, the receiver of complaint, plea and a wide range of bids for action and attention. In the processes of renewal and change now taking place the authority vested in him by his employers is of little assistance. He must continue to exercise his usual functions and he must also be clear that he shares a (to some minds) new role with teachers, a role expressed in its broadest terms as that of an *improver of education*. If it is, over all his functions, as an improver that he sees himself, his role in interaction with that of teachers will be less open to ambiguity. If both partners see themselves and each other in congruent roles, the first essential of partnership will have been achieved. But in finding this congruence it is the administrator who must take the first steps: if he fails to take the initiative in defining the relationship, he will risk his contribution being interpreted as authoritarian. Neither the teacher by virtue of any special expertness in handling the basic material of education nor the administrator by virtue of any vested authority in the organisation of support can afford to think of himself as all-knowing. When a broad programme of curriculum renewal is to be attempted there are no unquestioned experts.

When the administrator and the teacher know what to expect of one another, the administrator has to identify those needs which constitute the specification for his part in the co-operative process. In the reappraisal of curriculum the teacher has, from what the pupil needs and from what his subject structure requires, to shape a balanced specification for his teaching; this he then translates into the needs which the administrator must meet. The specification to which the administrator will then work will define the resources, human, material and financial which he must procure to meet these needs.

While it might seem reasonable to attempt a description of a teacher's needs which would fit all types and stages of curriculum change and to attempt, from such a description, to devise a model procedure of how to meet them, the overlap of categories of support, whether available or required, whether tangible or moral, makes this difficult. The quality of interaction between teacher and administrator, too, will depend on so many individual differences that we can go little further at present than to suggest that the administrator has a five-fold responsibility: to elicit a response to curriculum change from individual teachers (assistant teachers as well as heads), to help teachers to promote within themselves a well-informed confidence in their capacity for change, to assist in promoting co-operation and interaction among individual teachers (both in the same and in different schools), to organise resources and support from outside schools, and to be, himself, responsibly involved in the process of change.

The most difficult point in overt co-operation may well be the first move to get anything started at all: administrators are familiar with the situation in which teachers express a wish, though no more, to try something new: primary school French is perhaps already a classic example of a subject in which many teachers, admittedly with little to go on, evinced a wish to get started long before organised curriculum support was available. The Certificate of Secondary Education placed teachers in a rather similar position: after the publication of the Beloe Report there was an expectation that something had to happen, and that teachers themselves had to make it happen. But, as in primary French, additional support had first to come from an unknown source. In many authorities it was administrators and inspectors who, with teachers, provided a quick *ad hoc* framework for experiment and discussion. Within that framework teachers set their own aims and their own timetables. For such a framework to be devised proved an adequate stimulus to subsequent action.

The urge of inspiration, the appropriate stimulus for the teacher to act, will differ from subject to subject and from school to school. To ask the administrator to ensure that a broad range of stimuli is available is to ask for what is almost impossible: for who knows which other teacher, which outside speaker, which book, which conversation will unlock a teacher's latent energy and interest? Guesswork and administrative intuition might suffice but there are also reasonably well documented descriptions of the origins of innovation (for instance Pellegrin, 1966; Carlson, 1965a; Goldhammer, 1965; Clark and Guba, 1968). A crude codification of origins as manipulative, or moralistic, or prestigious or, simply, experimental may be helpful. While, for instance, it may be legitimate to give a first impetus to new thinking by issuing an authoritative request or challenge to the heads of schools, this would become discredited if it were a continuous policy. It would seem unlikely that an administrator who cared so little for congruence between his role and that of teachers that he tried, for example, continuously to bully innovation along would get very far. Similarly, to manipulate (as from a position of superiority) partners into a commitment from which they could not extricate themselves without the fear of losing professional face would call for a high but dubious skill: manipulation alone could hardly succeed for long. Again, to engineer an artificial prestige for new work is to risk the disaffection of, perhaps, the majority of teachers: deliberately to pour limelight only on the few is to give others an uncomfortable feeling of gloom. But while no one method will guarantee success in starting a process by which teachers can take and can sustain initiatives, it is important to consider stimuli at an early stage. The need can perhaps best be met by the administrator helping, in whatever way he can, the teachers to find for themselves their own best spurs to action.

Models for the organisation of initiative from other countries tend to assume an authoritarian power structure in the administration of education: consequently they are unhelpful for the British administrator. He must at this stage continue to rely on an approach which is empirical and which calls for the exercise of a personal and a thoughtful skill. For those who lack that skill the best hope might be that their influence in this activity remains limited until they know more about it.

But if the onus for finding the appropriate stimulus rests finally with the teacher, three other needs can only be met by a very free interchange between those, the teachers, who can refine their statement of need and those who can help towards an access to more specialised assistance. An essential in any reform in which the initiative must come from the one who is also the ultimate user is the ability to ask for and to take criticism. If a teacher has tried a new unit of work with one class, and if it appears successful, the reasonable next step is to try it in another setting, with other pupils, or in the hands of another teacher. Use of one's own work by other people means that comment, judgment, condemnation or modification is inevitable. Because there is no tradition of the teacher in Britain making his own work visible and accessible to other teachers he may need some assistance, and assistance not given by an outsider (as, for instance, the inspector may well be regarded) but by other teachers. It is the administrator's task to assist in ensuring that criticism by others finds a mode which is neither destructive nor over-threatening: it is his task, too, to ensure that interchange of ideas among schools and between the proposer and the critic is easy, informal and yet serious.

The comparison of new work between both teachers and schools has to be arranged: if one man's idea can only be effectively tried out by his working in the same classroom, workshop or laboratory as another with a similar interest in another school, the administrator has to ensure that the visit, perhaps on an extended basis of regular half-days, is made possible with no loss to either school. This is a matter of teacher supply, and, particularly, of ensuring either that an appropriate teacher is available as a substitute or that a school is able at the appropriate time (for a genuine rather than a fabricated purpose) to dispose its pupils in groups larger than that of one class. In the long process of curriculum renewal this would not be an *ad hoc* need but something for which systematic provision, with good planning, would be essential.

Again, the administrator has to work very closely with schools to meet any need which is expressed for a familiarity with, and confidence in, specialist techniques of, for example, measurement or evaluation. The long-term answer may be the training of an increasing number of serving teachers in research methods, but training schemes would produce, at best, only a trickle of those with a very thorough familiarity of research and development. But little that is not random, intuitive, and perhaps short-lived in its usefulness can be expected to emerge from curriculum reform unless teachers have a sufficient contact with those who work in more academically rigorous fields. It is important for teachers to look, for example, at research and to believe in its necessity, to respect it without being dazzled, and to know when it is, and when it is not, necessary to submit their own work to thorough analysis and appraisal. The staffs of institutes of education and some members of the staffs of colleges of education alone at present provide local sources of such expertness. An administrator needs, by working closely with these institutions, to be able to create such bridges as schools might not be able to build for themselves. A wider reference, too, to university departments of education and to faculty workers in other disciplines is a further dimension within which the administrator should seek to work.

In contrast to those areas of need in which only joint action can succeed, there are others where the administrator can aim only at helping teachers to provide for themselves: a self-critical approach to objectives, methods and achievement lies within one such area. It is a precaution for the teacher to be able to rely on his own appraisal of his treatment both of existing and of new elements in curriculum. But for the administrator to help to provide experience in those techniques of teachers' self-appraisal which have already been pioneered (for instance Flanders, 1965; Bush and Allen, 1964) requires a delicacy and sure-footedness which can only come from a familiarity both with the problems and with some, at least, of the techniques themselves. It requires that the administrator should mediate between professionals who do not normally meet; teachers on the one hand and, on the other, experts from such fields as, notably, sociology and psychometrics. Opportunities for direct contact may be few but much could be learned by the making available of reports on such work as has already been done elsewhere. Here the administrative task is to explore how far teachers believe (or can be brought to a belief) in the need for familiarity with techniques of self-assessment. Even if the administrator risks getting nowhere, the attempt to promote a heightened self-awareness in the professional teacher is a fitting parallel to the administrator's own need for self-scrutiny.

On the more mundane level, the administrator has a direct access to needed resources. In the initial stages of systematic curriculum change less money will be needed: later sophistication may bring demands for equipment, or for extensive visitations, or for increased aid in the classroom. But the principal investment in the early stages is in skill and in energy. When money is needed for materials, for lecture fees, for film, for transport, it should be immediately available; it should not involve the school in delay or uncertainty about whom to ask, or how to ask. The bureaucracy of control should be carefully minimised. Similarly, when teachers know (and here they may need to be helped to see how much they can ask for without being swamped) to whom they can turn for assistance—to Institutes, to colleges, to specialist associations, to national project teams, to the B.B.C. or I.T.A. or to publishers—quick administrative help in getting them in touch with the right man at the right time calls for skill, knowledge and a sense of urgency. At this stage, teachers may need encouragement to ask for help; to mediate in these pleas, to control, and to encourage this particularly calls, from the man in the middle, for foresight and a wide range of contacts.

Time is another resource which to some extent lies within the administrator's control, at least to the extent that it is his task to ensure that the work of re-appraisal is not carried on exclusively in the participant's private hours. Curriculum reform is a long job: it will not be separate projects, whatever their duration, which will be the most important part of the process: it will be the teacher's preparedness to undertake the responsibility of long-term professional self-renewal. Because it is a professional responsibility, paid time which is planned and provided for must be found. In times of teacher shortage the setting aside of a small regular period each week is difficult but essential, and particularly for the activities of teachers' centres, for teacher discussion, for lectures, and for practical work.

All these needs call for the administrator to share, with those who are directly concerned, in an investigation of all the factors which make up that internal mechanism of the school which supports the curriculum. The allocation of staff time, the allocation of rooms—these are the responsibility, in timetabling, of the school itself. But financial allowances, library resources, teachers' centres, inter-school visits, all these and more have an effect on the time, energy and sympathy which the teacher will devote to work in the advancement of change. The teacher who is isolated from sources of support is less likely to work confidently and effectively than the one who is given the sense that there is community of effort, that what he starts will continue to gain support as well as interest.

IV

The administrator's own very personal involvement in the process of change brings into play his resources of education and of experience as well as his resources of intellect, stamina and skill. If the administrator lacks the energy to retain an interest in, and a sense of the importance of, continuing and well-synthesised change, he will not be sensitive to the fluctuations in morale to which the process is prey: he may miss the signs which show that the goals of the effort are spaced too far apart, and which show that apathy results from too little a sense of achievement within short spans of effort. It is important for the administrator to stand sufficiently far back to notice the signs which indicate the state of morale; he alone can place himself in such a position without the risk of isolation from that process.

V

If the teacher is the principal agent of change, the focal points at which change occurs lie beyond the teacher; they include, most obviously, the pupil. But, beyond the teacher and the pupil, the content and method of learning as well as the materials and facilities which support learning are points in themselves at which the pressure of change has to be applied. The inter-relationship between the learner and what is learned is fostered by the teacher. But if learning is fostered increasingly in a climate in which the teacher is held to account and even if schooling, in its protected condition, is not something for which account is called in any context of competition or of profit, the providers of schooling are positively responsible to the several communities to which the child belongs. In particular, the family and the parent can either support or frustrate both the normal processes of schooling and the overhaul of those processes. Recent evidence exists of the measurable extent to which good or bad family support can influence a child's achievement (C.A.C.E., 1967): similarly attitudinal evidence exists (Schools Council 1968) of the degree to which some teachers find themselves and their work positively excluded from the process by which the family brings its young from infancy to adulthood: to connect teacher, school and home has an obvious importance. It is not enough to exhort the teacher to make the connection if nothing but crisis brings the parent into contact with the school system. If change at school is not to be distrusted (and perhaps discredited) at home, it would appear of high priority for the

138

administrator to ensure that schools can effectively transmit and ultimately share an awareness of the objectives of the school with the community. Whether the implicit conception of the school's role is that of shaping or of serving the community, little can be possible in winning over some larger part of the influences which affect school achievement unless a climate can exist in which the administrator can help the school to a confident view of its own accountability. This means that the school has not only to state the objectives but to provide for the communities from which its pupils come some commentary both on the methods used to achieve them and on the progress made towards them. To secure improvement in education involves the administrator not only in discerning and supporting the needs of teachers but also, in an atmosphere free of community pressures, in a narrowly political sense, in evolving and explaining a shared strategy for that improvement.

The acceptance of a strategy within which parents can assess their own degree of commitment for the support of teaching change exposes the administrator to a number or ill-defined pressures. The continual wash of public utterance, both exhortatory and recriminatory, about quality and about standards finds a more specialised voice in pleas for preparation for a technological society, for an increase, and better balance, in the number of university places, for foresight in coping with automated employment, for compensatory education for the deprived, for special consideration for gifted children, for an answer to, or at least an accommodation with, the mass media, and for the avoidance of the risks of producing a better educated but submerged social minority. Each exhortation inevitably assumes a background of change in societal modes of conduct, thought, or aspiration. Each, too, could (if allowed) make a difference to curriculum. To look beyond the locality and to gauge the practical importance to curriculum of such pleas is difficult enough: to make sense of these larger needs, to interpret them in a credible manner, and to connect them, in curricular terms, with local expectations of what a school can provide is almost too big a task. It is certainly too big for one man or even for one section of the system. But to make the interpretation and to attempt a connection between societal

139

need and curriculum is, again, a task upon which no one other than the administrator is as well placed to embark. To interpret education too narrowly to society (and vice versa) carries too great a risk. The administrator has to be sensitive to the breadth of demand.

In attempting to provide a means of mediation between the broader concerns of society and the more obvious expectations of one locality, the administrator has to identify and to listen to those who express both kinds of concern: the teacher sees a picture different from that of the educator of teachers and the industrialist or the commercial employer sees a different picture again: the universities have yet another view. To put it another way,

...there has been insufficient cross fertilisation of ideas and experience between government, industry, trade unions and the educational system and...there has been excessive compartmentalisation between the different sectors of our national life (Shanks, 1967).

In one sense a synopsis of differing perspectives should be found in the lay committee, but it seems doubtful whether many education committees can achieve or attempt to achieve this. But if administration is to concern itself with improvement and if the administrator is in any way to make a contribution which can help towards deciding between priorities in curriculum, he must allow himself the time to bring the views of others to bear upon the work.

To organise an interplay between the local education authority and the community is part of the prescribed function of local administration: to organise an interaction open enough to allow society's values to have a weight in the choice of what is taught and to encourage that interaction to the point of bringing change about is to go beyond the prescribed function. But to create a situation which is so open as to bring instability to the organisation of a local education authority is a risk which any organisation must face which needs to maintain itself in a steady state. To encourage change which directly affects teachers and which, later and less directly, affects pupils, parents and employers (as well as the other users of education) means awakening a response. This response to change should affect the subsequent activities of the administrator. If the feedback cannot be controlled within the norms of administration, disruption follows. (And, since the norms are not generally dictated by the need for innovation, this is a real risk.) Both the efficiency and the morale of the administrator might be badly damaged.

VI

To change the curriculum is neither simple nor safe, for if it is done well it has (for this should be its aim) to change the quality of the society under whose aegis it is provided. The administrator has to be aware of which parts of his administration are exposed to the risk of destructive pressure: the sub-system of inspectors and advisers, for instance, is exposed to a greater risk, perhaps, than that of the clerical, precedent-following control system, or than that of the part precedent-bound, part initiatory executive sub-system. And the pressures of disruption are unlikely to be foreseeable until we know much more about the process of change.

In meeting the need to ensure maximum stability with a maximum openness to the initiative as well as to the feedback of other partners in curriculum change the administrator has to be sure of his personal position. Status, age, experience, academic background, temperament and energy all are obviously relevant. While parallels from the United States are difficult either to draw or to follow and while little that is true of the community-cum-political setting of the school district superintendency is true of the local education authority, there are well evidenced (and not very obscure) conclusions which can both go beyond assertion and can claim some credibility in Britain. At the least, the implications of points which we may tacitly assume but which we never openly acknowledge are worth considering. If an authority cannot support change unless it changes itself, what is the significance of, for instance, statements about the age, status, length of tenure of office, or hierarchical inclinations of senior administrators (Griffiths, 1964; Carlson, 1965b)?

There is a case, in Britain, for considering the implications of such simple things as the age and status of the administrators and for considering the advantages and disadvantages of the uniquely British style of local hierarchy. We could be clearer about the feasibility of giving an appropriate weight in the local plan of school change to those social and other factors which vary in their importance from decade to decade. But what emerges even from the most cursory examination of the administration of curriculum change is that we know very little that is systematic either of the theory or of the practice of such administration in Britain.

VII

When the knowledge base of any activity is weak it has to be strengthened—by research, by enquiry and by the observation and recording of planned action. The present time is appropriate for the beginnings of a four-fold plan of action. We need to know in an accessible and intelligible form what research is currently being carried out into the many aspects of change-administration: we need to know the literature of past research: we need to have some description of how change is handled in local education authorities now and we need to know of good practice, not of bad. Finally, we need to find out how, by a synthesis of theory and practice, we can make a composite statement about the administration of change which, while useful in the preparation of new administrators, shows, too, where the gaps are in our knowledge. Because we have no methods of preparing administrators for their work there is little risk that what would result from such a plan would be divorced from reality. The in-service education of administrators falls well behind the quality and scope of that which we provide for teachers. It would be bizarre to stress the need for teacher retraining in the face of change and at the same time to ignore those who can do most to help or hinder the process of change itself.

Bibliography

Baron, G. and Tropp A. (1961) 'Teachers in England and America', in Halsey, Floud and Anderson (eds.) *Education, Economy, and Society*, New York: The Free Press of Glencoe.

Bush, R. and Allen, D. (1964) *Controlled Practice in the Training of Teachers*, Secondary Education Project, School of Education, Stanford University, mimeographed.

Carlson, R.O. (1965a) 'Barriers to Change in Public Schools', in Carlson (ed.) *Change Processes in Public Schools*, Eugene: Center for the Advanced Study of Educational Administration, University of Oregon.

Carlson, R.O. (1965b) *Adoption of Educational Innovations*, Eugene: Center for the Advanced Study of Educational Administration, University of Oregon.

Central Advisory Council for Education (England) (1967) *Children and their Primary Schools*, London: H.M.S.O.

Clarke, D.L. and Guba, E.G. (1969) 'Effecting Change in Institutions of Higher Education', in Baron, G., Cooper, D., Walker, W.G. (eds.) *Educational Administration: International Perspectives*, Chicago: Rand McNally.

Flanders, N.A. (1965) *Teacher Influence, Pupil Attitudes, and Achievement*, Co-operative Research Monograph No. 12, Washington: U.S. Department of Health, Education and Welfare.

Goldhammer, K. (1965) *Issues and Strategies in the Public Acceptance of Educational Change*, Eugene: Center for the Advanced Study of Educational Administration, University of Oregon.

Griffiths, D.E. (1964) 'Administrative Theory and Change in Organisations', in Miles, M.B. (ed.) *Innovation in Education*, New York: Bureau of Publications, Teachers College, Columbia University.

Pellegrin, R.J. (1966) *An Analysis of Sources and Processes of Innovation in Education*, Eugene: Center for the Advanced Study of Educational Administration, University of Oregon.

Schools Council (1968) *Enquiry I: Young School Leavers*, London: H.M.S.O.

Shanks, M. (1967) *The Innovators*, London: Penguin Books.

Chapter 8

Administration and Educational Technology

K. Austwick

Towards a Technology of Education

Educational technology is an emotive expression tending to produce an excess of attitude striking. Self-styled liberals or progressives clutch their children about them ready to defend to the death the personal element of education—the direct human contact between teacher and taught, the so-called meeting of minds; whilst taxonomists, systems analysts, the white-coated faceless ones, reduce education to a collection of measurables—a predictable, controllable, automated process in which the child passes through a clinically controlled environment to emerge at the end duly charged and docketed. The popular image of educational technology is of gadgetry, whether audio-visual aids, computers or dinner ticket and milk dispensers. To the writer, educational technology, or better the technology of education, implies an applied science, or if you like, the application of sciences to education. Precisely which sciences are involved is a matter for experiment—certainly one would include sociology and psychology, lighting, printing and photography, acoustics and electronics, but perhaps increasingly we must consider management, architecture and building science, ergonomics, systems analysis and communications.

The task of building a complete technology of education—the study of sciences applicable in the field of education—would seem to be as yet in its infancy. In fact this wider interpretation might seem to presume administration as a part of the field rather than an independent factor as implied by the title of this chapter. Perhaps we should start from the more popular current image which incorporates audio-visual and other teaching aids, and perhaps building design, and consider later the wider implications. The interaction of administration and educational technology may be regarded as a two-stage problem reflecting a recurring pattern which can be exemplified in the phrase 'adapt–adopt' as used by Lange (1967).

With the development of speech, of writing, of printing, of photography, of sound recording and reproduction, and more recently of motion film and television, the teaching–learning process has first *adapted* new skills or materials designed in other spheres. Later their influence becomes so pervasive that the process or system has to *adopt* the philosophy of the new in preference to the old. Thus in the Socratic or tutorial situation, face to face confrontation was of the essence. The development of writing and later of printing first provided material to supplement the existing pattern. Dialogue was related to material stored in manuscript form. Later the fuller potential of the new media became clear.

The student could learn via the book, with or without the teacher, before or after meeting him. Information could be stored outside the teacher and transported at will. The pattern of teaching and learning changed, acquiring a new dimension in both space and time; libraries and schools and universities emerged. More recently, film, radio, television, language laboratories and teaching machines have appeared, to be adapted in turn to suit the existing classroom teaching–learning situation. Blacking-out curtain is provided for the magic lantern or slide projector, a wireless receiver or loud speaker is installed in the classroom for radio broadcasts, tape recorders and teaching machines are installed on desks, television cameras are brought into the classroom or laboratory. In all these cases the new devices are being adapted to suit the needs of an existing situation. Even experiments with computers are tried on scheduling *existing* time-tables.

This is the 'adapting' stage.

But now we are perhaps moving towards the 'adoption' stage, and the teaching–learning process is being re-thought. Is television best used with larger groups, teaching machines and language laboratories on an individual basis? If so, what are the implications for the design of teaching and learning spaces and for organisational or administrative structures? Does the use of mass media lead naturally to team teaching and the redeployment of teaching manpower and skills? Should the teacher, the equipment, the aids and the buildings be regarded as a complete man-machine system in which all the parts must simultaneously be deployed to achieve an optimum level of operation for the benefit of the student? If so, what are the objectives of the total system—are they the same as those of earlier days? How does the new technological situation interact with the desired socio-logical pattern to meet today's demand for the education of large numbers of children working under one roof? Can the educational advantages of individualised programmes be matched with the social claims for the large or comprehensive unit? What are the administrative implications?

Teaching Aids and Group Size

The first and most obvious area of application of educational technology is in teaching aids and media, which in turn affect methods of teaching and the grouping and accommodating of children for teaching and learning purposes. These are all factors *within* the school, and it is here that the chain of events begins. Administration can be treated at three levels—national, local and school, and the effects of the new technology filter from schools to local and to national levels. For instance, local educa-tion authorities are now appointing advisers in educational technology as well as participating in, or sponsoring, experi-ments in schools. At the national level, we have had the Bryn-mor Jones report on audio–visual aids in higher education leading to the establishment of a National Council for Educa-tional Technology. Independent organisations like the Nuffield Foundation, which has sponsored a Resources for Learning project, are also contributing, and the Department of Education and Science has its Educational Technology section.

Let us look first at the school situation and consider in some detail, at ground level, attempts to adapt technological aids into the existing system. It is worth noting initially that the many aids appearing in schools are particularly appropriate either to large group or to individualised instruction rather than to the conventional class group to which we are accustomed. We will therefore consider one or two cases at each end of this group-size spectrum, in particular programmed learning and language laboratories on the one hand and television on the other. In the case of programmed learning the comments are based on experimental work involving several classes of approximately thirty-five children using teaching machines in a school near Bath, one purpose of the study being to consider the organisational problems arising at classroom level.

Programmed learning, or self-instruction in the field of written material, may be presented in machine or book form. The material is subjected to a detailed analysis and then presented in small units, in such a way that the pupil can teach himself. The student must make some response or answer to each item presented to him. Each response is assessed and the pupil's progress is determined in the light of his response—going forward if correct and repeating a step or receiving additional help if incorrect. In a conventional text larger amounts of subject matter are presented at a time with an assumption that the student will probably receive help and advice from a teacher, whereas the programmed text attempts to provide a self-sufficient piece of instruction—in other words not only subject matter but a teaching method as well. As a result programmed learning in book form requires a longer text to cover the same amount of material as would be covered in a shorter text of the conventional type and hence is more expensive. In addition the volume of storage space taken up is correspondingly larger (two factors which militate against its adoption within normal school budgets). Programmes take up less storage space and suffer less wear and tear if they are on film; but this implies they are presented in a teaching machine of some description, and the teaching machine itself presents problems of storage and maintenance. Many of the multiple-choice type of programmes, for instance, make use of teaching machines for their presentation, and these can be the size of a small television set. Such machines are costly for schools to purchase and so renting systems for limited periods have been developed by the manufacturers—with consequent insurance problems! We find, therefore, immediate problems of budgeting, storage and maintenance.

Schools in general are organised on the basis of class sizes of about thirty-five, but it is a major operation to provide thirty-five teaching machines and to accommodate them. The problem is less serious in a technical college, where classes may be smaller or more diverse and a small number of teaching machines may suffice, but in a school the provision of a set of thirty-five such machines means that the conventional classroom is very much overloaded with equipment, and space becomes a problem. In addition, power supplies are required and many conventional classrooms have only a few power points. If these are to take a large number of machines then some planning is necessary to cater for the variations in power requirement of the machines; for instance, in setting up the type of machine which back-projects film on to a screen the power required is greatest when the machine is first switched on. If a large number of machines are to be used this operation cannot proceed simultaneously on all the machines and therefore appropriate organisation at the beginning of the lesson is required. Further problems arise with this type of machine in making use of a film in that the buttons used to move the film frames can be noisy (although from experiments with children this noise factor does not seem to cause undue concern to the children themselves). The setting up of a battery of such machines is time-consuming and therefore it is likely that the room in which they are housed will not be available for any other purpose over a period of time.

This produces time-tabling difficulties. There are further problems occasioned by the fact that schools are based on fixed time units for lessons, whereas children work at their own speed through programmed learning and hence complete pro-grammes at different times. Similarly students who are part-way through a programme at the end of the lesson time will have to break off and resume at a later stage. Does this mean that the machine must lie idle until the same student returns and can take up where he left off? If not, the next student coming along may require a different programme, in which case the machine must be reloaded; or he may be working on the same programme but have reached a different point from the first student. In either case when the first student returns he must again either reload the film or at least search along it for his point of exit from the last lesson. If this is to be done, either the teacher must do it for each child, which would take an impos-sible amount of time, or the children must be given additional instruction in how to do the operation for themselves (an additional and, in a sense, irrelevant skill). Programmes are often supplied with criterion tests which the student should take at the end of a programme and he must have access to these quickly and easily. Moreover they must be organised so that there is time to complete a test within a given lesson; the test has to be marked in order that the student's next course of action can be determined in the light of his performance on the criterion tests of the programme that he has just completed. These are areas of administrative difficulty unless the tests can be marked objectively by clerks or other teacher ancillaries. In summary then, to introduce programmed learning and teaching machines produces administrative problems for the school as a whole—budgeting, storage, maintenance, time-tabling, clerical help—and problems in the classroom—power supplies, accommodation, test marking, student counselling and organisation of machine operation. In other words, there are administrative problems at two levels—school and classroom.

Let us turn next to the language laboratory. Here again there is a problem of class size. The purpose of the language laboratory is, amongst other things, to enable the student to work at his own speed and it is necessary for him to assess his own progress. This, however, must be overseen by the teacher who monitors the activity of his class members and communicates with them. Since the students are progressing at different speeds they will reach the end of items of instruction at different times. In order to have adequate control over a class, a group size of perhaps twelve would be ideal for a teacher so that he could give adequate attention to each member. This, however, would represent considerably less than half of a normal class unit. The school is then immediately faced with the problem of what to do with the other half, since teaching staff must be available to attend to their needs. On the other hand if a class unit of conventional size works in a language laboratory one has gone half-way back to the conventional classroom situation of trying to teach a group of thirty-five, perhaps by oral methods, and being able to involve only a limited number at a time. If we have a language laboratory catering for thirty-five students the amount of time that can be given to each student is markedly reduced and the purpose of using the language laboratory to some extent defeated. Again, a room equipped as a language laboratory is immobilised as far as most other forms of teaching are concerned, and implies a constraint on the time-table to an even greater extent than in the case of a battery of teaching machines, which are at least removable in an emergency. The presence of an expensively equipped room also places some pressure on a school's administrators to seek maximum usage of the equipment, which may lead to a tendency to teach by this method whether appropriate or not, simply to ensure 'economic' use.

Another serious problem, particularly applicable to the language laboratory but also to some extent to the more complicated teaching machine, is the question of maintenance. A language laboratory with a teacher console and thirty or forty student stations is bound to produce maintenance problems when individual booths may be out of action. Even one booth out of action, implying one child surplus to the number which the laboratory can cater for, produces immediately administrative difficulties in a class, and there is an implication that a competent technician should be on hand virtually at all times. This, then, implies problems of administration in so far as non-academic staff in a school or institution are concerned. Should we seek technicians who are competent not only to work in school science laboratories and in craft workshops, but who are also competent to handle the electronics of a language laboratory? Such people are not likely to be available in large numbers. The alternative is to have technicians particularly competent in the field of servicing electronic equipment, and many schools may not be able to afford this. On the other hand they may not be able to afford a language laboratory which does not operate reliably or at full efficiency! Does this call into question the wisdom of a set of schools each provided with a full range of science laboratories, language laboratories, workshops, teaching machines and so on, or should some concentration of resources between schools be sought—always assuming of course that this would not be interpreted as implying some form of 'selection' as opposed to comprehension!

Finally there is a problem of materials for both language laboratory and the teaching machines.

Supplies of tapes and programmed learning are limited. Is it then the function of a teacher to manufacture his own or to purchase these commercially? Purchasing them commercially would be expensive. On the other hand, if a teacher is to manufacture his own he will need time to do this, which presumably must be taken from a normal teaching load, and he may well require some technical assistance in production and testing. This again has time-tabling and staff scheduling implications.

Implications

We have taken two particular cases of individualised teaching, viz. teaching machines and language laboratories, to draw attention to some new administrative problems which arise when these new aids are introduced into a school pattern not originally designed to cater for them, and in which the system and the new teaching aids have to be adapted in some sort of a compromise to make use of the aids feasible.

School time-tables are based on fixed time units or modules. We do not teach to specified levels or criteria so much as for given time intervals. Allowing students full scope to work at their own speeds over a specified content of material conflicts with the concept of working for specified time intervals and produces serious problems in planning student schedules. In fact this has led to some experimenting on the use of group pacing techniques with teaching machines in an attempt to adapt the new method to the existing administrative framework.

The two aids have also produced budgeting problems in that they are costly in comparison with other teaching materials; problems of storage in that they immobilise space in schools; and problems of material and supply in that many items on the market are not compatible with each other (although attempts are being made to standardise teaching machines). Finally, they imply the need for additional operatives within schools—technicians, clerical assistants, possibly graphic and photographic experts. Pressures of these kinds tend to polarise teachers' attitudes—either to reject the aids or to demand large-scale re-planning of the whole school system.

Similar problems will also arise with the introduction of large group teaching systems like closed circuit television, where there is need not only for technical assistance with the equipment but also professional advice on performance in front of television cameras, the provision of graphics and other materials to assist in the television presentation itself and the determination of optimum group sizes for efficient and effective use of such resources.

These examples indicate the problems which are arising with attempts to adapt new technological devices to the teaching situation, and which will in time produce pressures requiring the whole situation to be re-thought. It is also worth bearing in mind that with the introduction of programmed learning, of language laboratory tapes, and of outside broadcasts, or even of closed circuit television between one school and another, students are receiving pre-packaged lessons and that the teacher in effect is becoming a sort of intermediary between his class and another teacher elsewhere. This was well illustrated with the introduction of schools' television broadcasting. Initially this was designed as 'enrichment'—in other words to supplement or extend the existing courses provided by the teacher. Later, in view of the shortage of teachers in subjects such as mathematics, and of the introduction of new content into school courses, the broadcasts began to take the form of direct teaching. This implies an appreciable change of role on the part of the teacher. The present situation is one in which the teacher integrates pre-packaged lessons into his own programme, but the question must of course arise whether at a later stage there may be a reversal of these roles. One is only too familiar with the school problem of the shortage of specialist teachers; and the fact that the few available tend to come and go in any one school with distressing frequency. Will the time soon come when heads will plan courses in terms of the available 'canned' teaching from television, programmed learning and other sources and expect these 'short-term' staff to fit into such an overall scheme?

From 'Adapt' to 'Adopt'

We have considered so far some of the specific problems which can arise in adapting new technological devices as teaching aids.

In particular we have considered programmed learning and teaching machines, the language laboratory and television. In each case the new aid provides opportunity for enhancing the teaching or learning situation but exacts its price in administrative complications. The combined effect of these aids is to assault the concept of one-teacher-one-class and the fixed time unit of instruction. We are bound to consider whether children should always work in standard sized classes or whether they would be better off working part of their time in large groups and other times working on their own. The administrative problems in scheduling such a programme for children are considerable. We should also consider how to define the roles of the teacher. Is he a subject matter expert, is he a counsellor, is he a mediator between the pupil and some pre-programmed instruction brought in from elsewhere? Should teachers spend part of their time working in teams rather than in their conventional individual role? Further, we must consider how far new buildings can be planned to cater for new aids and media, for the additional non-academic staff likely to be involved, and for the new roles and activities of the teacher?

It then becomes necessary to reconsider what are the objectives of the educational system, how are these to be achieved, how one can assess whether they are in fact being achieved, how the most efficient use can be made of the resources available, and how the system can be designed so as to take account of further possible change.

We have seen that attempts to adapt new technological devices as learning/teaching aids into the existing system produce formidable administrative problems: so much so that their use as aids will be inhibited unless we are prepared to go beyond the stage of *adapting* technological products, to that of *adopting* a technological approach to the school situation. For instance, programmed learning has brought with it the approach to course work of the behavioural scientist—the specification of objectives, the determination of criteria to assess terminal behaviours, and so on—leading to a technology of instruction (Wallis, 1966). In the same way in the wider context we may approach a technology of education by asking: What are the objectives of the system, how do we determine criteria to assess their achievement, what resources are available and how do we deploy them?

The Total System

It is perhaps appropriate in this context to look at the total system of buildings, equipment, aids, teaching strength and the supply of students, and the relationship of these to the socio-economic background of the neighbourhood. If buildings are being designed from scratch they must reflect the philosophy and objectives of the institution. They must also take cognisance of the servicing requirements of its various departments which may lead to new groupings of subject rooms; for instance, where language teaching requires the use of a laboratory it may well be more appropriate to station this nearer to the other types of laboratory and/or workshops, whereas more traditional language teaching was likely to be located in a classroom block. The development of teaching aids and all the materials which go with these may well imply the need for some central service unit, probably associated with the library, where tapes, film-strip, programmes and so on can be stored and if necessary prepared. Such a centre needs to be geographically easily accessible to the whole of the school and may well require technical and clerical staff on a larger scale than at present.

It also becomes necessary to consider the functions performed by the teacher since a new division of these may be more appropriate; for instance, amongst other things, teachers may be regarded as subject matter stores, stores of teaching skills, and stores of information about students. Some teachers are better information stores than others, some are more adept at communicating with students than others, and some are particularly successful in the sphere of pastoral care.

It may be necessary to recognise these individual differences in the allocation of roles to various teachers, and this may in turn imply development of team teaching conditions. Teachers are already identified with particular roles. It is worth recalling how the special responsibility salary allowances introduced during the 1950's were particularly concerned with additional payments to the subject matter experts. In the evolution of comprehensive schools allowances are being paid to house masters—in other words payments are being made to teachers exercising a pastoral-care role. The introduction of new aids, as already mentioned, is creating a further change of role for the teacher. Modern aids make use of prepared and pre-packaged items of instruction and this places the teacher in the role of a mediator between his students and the programme writer or planner. The more able teachers may also be the programme creators. In this case their own time-table or work programme will be very different from their current ones. Time and facilities will be needed for preparation of material, be it tapes, teaching machine programmes or television presentations.

It is also necessary to determine how far a student's individual needs affect the planning of his programme and the extent to which he can be provided with individual self-instruction, how far he can be provided with pre-packed lessons and how far he needs the services of a live teacher. In terms of the student's personality it might be possible to determine how he should distribute his time between individualised instruction, small group and large group working. We are already familiar with the evidence advanced against streaming, which suggests that, in academic terms, the good may get better but the poor get poorer. If we match teaching methods to such personality factors as introversion/extroversion, shall we be in danger of magnifying these personality differences—and does it matter?

If teachers are to perform a greater counselling role they will need guidance as to how best to advise students, how best to match the student's needs and the school's resources. In this, as in the other areas discussed above, the teacher not only needs access to but should also assist by contributing to research findings and innovation.

In the longer term it may be appropriate to consider how far the student's presence in school itself is essential, whether his education can be carried on partly outside the walls of the school. If this proved possible it might be feasible to develop a shift system, whereby pupils were in school only for certain parts of the day. This is not entirely inconsistent with some of the recommendations of the Newsom report.

Administration

Perhaps the following quote from Clark Trow (1963) best summarises the categories of problems we have outlined:

> Organizing the curriculum and instruction will include more irregularities than now, and new sources. Staff utilization will present more complex problems in view of the differentiation of function, and will necessitate provision for more specialised training than at present; while planning and organizing learning resources, schedules, and work spaces will be an exacting task, but a rewarding one. The principal or superintendent will have the responsibility for making policy decisions and will have to work out the complicated arrangements for groups of different sizes meeting for periods of different lengths. Further they will be in charge of a more diversified staff than at present, staff assistants including clerks and technicians, staff specialists, and subject matter specialists.

To co-ordinate this wide array of variables—subject matter, teachers, pupils, aids, buildings—implies impressive administrative problems, the resolution of which would almost certainly require computer facilities. Experiments in computer scheduling of time-tables at M.I.T. have been sufficiently successful for contracts to be undertaken to schedule high school programmes in various parts of the United States. One such experiment was launched in 1962 at the Ridgewood High School in Chicago, where teaching is conducted in large groups, seminars and laboratory classes and where teachers work in teams and students are allowed a wide range of subject choices (Murphy, 1964). More recently, studies have been conducted in this country, for instance by the Local Government Operational Research Unit, into school and university time-tabling (Britten and Groom, 1967; see also Myers, Chapter 9). Reference is made in the L.G.O.R.U. publication to the conflict between class-based and student-based concepts of time-tabling—with a preference for the class-based system! But it would seem clear that the new technological aids cannot be comfortably adapted into the existing administrative and organisational set-up in schools since the conflict between current time modules and curriculum content modules, between the traditional framework of class instruction and individually scheduled student programmes may be too fundamental to be resolved adequately by makeshift or compromise.

Further areas of study and decision, in addition to time-tabling, which concern the administrator, are those of resources, staffing and students.

Taking these in turn: expenditure in the educational system is limited and new aids often seem very expensive when compared to more conventional teaching materials. On the other hand, many of these aids can perform some of the functions of a teacher in a way that the other materials do not, and might therefore come to be balanced against expenditure on teaching staff, and money for salaries greatly outweighs money for books and equipment at present. A shift of expenditure from labour to materials would pose some interesting dilemmas at local authority level.

The local administrator also needs technical advice on the purchase of equipment: on, for example, the choice between an expensive but versatile language laboratory and a cheaper and less versatile one; the critical point at which to purchase essential equipment in a falling price market (the cost of video tape recorders has dropped from thousands to hundreds of pounds over a period of a few years); or the problems presented by essential equipment which may well be obsolete long before it wears out.

In the field of personnel, reference has already been made to the demand for increased technical assistance in schools, some of which will have to be of high quality. Additional clerical or other aides may also be required, so that a school will become an institution employing a much wider range of staff, both academic and non-academic, with consequent increases in demarcation problems, conflict of roles, and an extending social hierarchy. Will schools in these situations have some need for personnel or welfare officers? Teachers may find themselves playing a series of diverse roles in team teaching, conventional teaching and as intermediaries, counsellors and retrainees. What will be the position of teachers who are unwilling or perhaps unable to cope with these sudden and varied roles?

Finally, with regard to the children, increased individualisation of programmes implies much more extensive and detailed

157

keeping of records and counselling. This factor has of course already arisen in primary schools as a result of informal or discovery methods. How far can the data collecting and processing be delegated by the teacher, and to whom or what?

Many of these problems are already arising, irrespective of the advent of complex teaching aids, and teachers are finding themselves taking on ever more tasks, many of which do not represent a sensible or economic use of their time, energies or skills. At this stage, the advent of educational technology would appear to be a source of yet more problems for administrators rather than a source of help in solving old ones!

Bibliography

Britten, A.A. and Groom, K.N. (1967) *The Use of Computers for School Timetabling*, Reading: Local Government Operational Research Unit.

Bushnell, D.D. and Allen, D.W. (1967) *The Computer in American Education*, New York: Wiley.

Bushnell, D.D. (ed.) (1964) *The Automation of School Information Systems*, Washington: National Education Association, Department of Audio-Visual Instruction.

Bushnell, D.D. (1963) *The Role of the Computer in Future Instructional Systems*, Audio Visual Communication Review, Washington: National Education Association, Department of Audio-Visual Instruction.

Coulson, J. (ed.) (1962) *Programmed Learning and Computer Based Instruction*, New York: Wiley.

Lange, P.C. (ed.) (1967) *Programmed Instruction*, 66th Year Book of the N.S.S.E., Chicago: University of Chicago Press.

Murphy, J. (1964) *School Scheduling by Computer*, New York: Educational Facilities Laboratories.

O.E.C.D. (1966) *Curriculum Improvement and Educational Development*, Paris: O.E.C.D.

Oettinger, A.G. (1966) *A Vision of Technology and Education*, Cambridge, Mass.: Harvard University Press.

Trow, W.C. (1963) *Teacher and Technology*, New York: Appleton-Century-Crofts.

Wallis, D. (March 1966) 'The Technology of Military Training', *Journal of the Royal Naval Scientific Service*, **21**, 2.

Chapter 9
Operational Research in Educational Administration
C. L. Myers

Introduction

Few people interested in educational administration could fail to grasp its affinity with say, economics or sociology. These are long established methodologies supported by many years of research and with obvious relevance to all types of administration. The case of Operational Research (O.R.) is somewhat different. In the country as a whole only a very small proportion have heard of it and of these only a minority will be aware of its relevance to the problems facing the educational administrator. The purpose of this paper is to extend that minority and to outline how, when and where O.R. techniques can be useful.

Basically O.R. can be defined as the application of scientific method to problems of management. This definition in turn begs two questions (at least!). What is meant by scientific method and what by problems of management?

Scientific Method

In this context, scientific method means three things:

(a) quantification
(b) logic
(c) model building.

O.R. usually involves measurement of some kind in order that the elements of a problem may be expressed in numerical terms and relationships established between them. It is these relationships that are often fundamental to resolving the problem for they enable the O.R. scientist to establish in logical terms a copy of the existing situation in all its important terms. This copy, 'the model', is the crux of O.R. It is possible to vary the elements within it and gauge the effect on objectives. Of course, the concept of a model is by no means new. The wind tunnel used for testing aircraft is a physical model and a more familiar example is the school timetable—a pencil and paper model simulating the movements of pupils and teachers. In O.R. models are usually mathematical although the mathematics may take the form of a single equation. Further example of models will be given later.

The Problem

Defining the problem properly is an important part of the O.R. approach. Such definition is rarely self-evident and involves careful understanding of the operation under study and a clear knowledge of the objectives it is trying to achieve. Fundamentally a problem of management occurs when the manager is faced with choosing between alternatives. Without choice there is no problem! It is all too easy to mistake symptoms for problems and in resolving the symptoms to leave the fundamental problems unsolved. For example, suppose the symptom that caused concern was the regularity of queues forming in a large canteen. One way to resolve this would be to raise the price of all meals served and so reduce custom. This, however, might not satisfy the objectives of the canteen which could be to maximise profits or increase the number of meals served, both of which tend to aggravate the symptoms. It is clear that whatever the objectives of the canteen any solution for alleviating the symptoms must be compatible with them.

One last point before leaving this definition of O.R. Essentially the power of O.R. techniques is wasted if the problems being studied are not reasonably complex. To use O.R. to decide whether to take an umbrella with you to work in the morning (a problem many find exceedingly difficult) is surely using a sledgehammer to crack a nut.

Operational Research Methods

Having loosely defined O.R., it is worth looking at its history. Basically, it started during the Second World War when the name was applied to research into the operations of the R.A.F. Since the war, every industrialised nation in the world has been increasing its use of Operational Research, and in particular the United States has a large number of O.R. scientists working in the universities and in industry, and advising the armed forces. In Britain the most notable developments have been in the nationalised industries, the steel industry and the oil companies. Now there are some two thousand O.R. scientists working in a variety of firms, public and private, of all types throughout the country. However, in government and in the social sciences generally, Operational Research appplications have, up to the last few years, been few. This situation is now changing and in this paper some examples are given where O.R. techniques are already helping educational administrators.

It is worth looking in detail, however, at the kind of problems O.R. has helped to resolve in industry, for it was with this back-ground that O.R. techniques have begun to be applied in the social sphere. With the passage of time, O.R. scientists have developed a number of special techniques for particular types of problems. Among these are queueing theory, network analysis, stock control methods, linear programming, dynamic program-ming and simulation (Duckworth, 1962; Rivett and Ackoff, 1963).

Queueing Theory is, as its name implies, used to study situations in which queues develop. The classical theory was originated by a Danish mathematician Erlang and related to queues that occur on telephone lines. Nowadays, queueing theory can be applied in respect of queues of people in canteens or queues of ships waiting to berth at docks. To solve these queueing problems statistical equations are formed which enable the chance of a given situation arising to be calculated. Solving these equations is often difficult unless the arrival and serving patterns conform to well known statistical theoretical distributions and for this reason queueing theory can only be used to solve the simpler queueing situations. In many traffic situations, for instance, the interactions are so complicated that analytical methods cannot be applied and, in this case, the scientist very often has to resort to 'simulation'.

Simulation is a generic term which could well be applied to almost all O.R. methods. By definition it means a representation and, of course, all model building is of this form. However, it is normally used in O.R. terminology to mean a model of a system specifically designed for experimentation. Many O.R. models are used with a small number of different values of the relevant parameters to establish the outcome of some alternative courses of action. Simulations, on the other hand, are 'run' several times (sometimes many hundreds) in order to estimate the likelihood of certain outcomes arising. This is because simulations are often applied in cases of uncertainty when relationships are not determined but could range over a series of values. An example of this would be traffic arriving at a traffic lights. The interval time between the first and second car arriving might range between 2 seconds and 85 seconds, the most frequent value being 15 seconds. In this case the single value (15 seconds) could not necessarily be used and the model would have to be 'operated' several times to see what happens if the value is 2 seconds, 5 seconds, 15 seconds, 60 seconds, etc. etc. This then is a characteristic of simulations—to be able to run them several times in order to get a fair reflection of what happens in practice. For this reason many simulations nowadays are designed for fast computers because these are far quicker than manual methods.

Simulations have a special use in management training. An effective simulation can represent in minutes operations that in real life could take months or years. In this way managers can have a 'dummy run' of the problem that they and other managers may have to face. A simulation program which is being used to train teachers is discussed in Taylor's contribution to this book. In industrial problems simulations are becoming more and more useful since so many cannot easily be resolved by the use of analytical mathematical equations.

Network Analysis is used for planning and scheduling work. The type of work to which it can be applied may be concrete and practical as in the building of a school or abstract as in the running of a research project. Basically Network Analysis breaks down the task under study into separate elements and puts them into a logical framework. In particular, it looks at which of the elements control completion of the project (i.e. which are 'critical') and determines, in the light of this the best way of planning (the 'critical path'). Two well known techniques are C.P.M. (Critical Path Method) and P.E.R.T. (Program Evaluation and Review Techniques). The latter, one of the first of these techniques, was originally devised for the planning of the Polaris Submarine programme. Nowadays the technique and variations of it are used widely in Britain and other major industrial countries.

Stock Control methods are used to control the amount of goods that have to be held in reserve in any warehouse situation; this includes the conventional supermarket where stock control is used to determine how much of each particular line to hold in stock and at what level the stock has to fall before a decision to re-order is made. Similarly, stock control can be used by local authority stores to determine how many school exercise books or pencils a store should have to be able to meet the demand from its customers, the individual schools.

Linear Programming is used to solve what is called an allocation problem. By this is meant a problem where there are a certain number of tasks to be performed which require resources. The resources provided are adequate to perform the tasks, but at least some of these can be done in a variety of different ways. Some ways are better than others but there are not enough resources available for the tasks to be performed if each is done in the best possible way. For example, consider the transportation of coal from the National Coal Board's pits to the Electricity Board's power stations. Each pit produces a certain amount of coal of a given quality, similarly each power station wants a certain amount of coal of each quality, and there is a cost attached to transporting the coal from pit to power station. Linear programming could be used to minimise the overall transport costs involved in this situation. The number of alternative solutions is very large and the best of these is not obvious. Consider, for example, starting with each pit serving only its nearest power station. Then it would be possible to end up with a power station a very long way away from any pit being short of coal and the overall cost of transportation consequently being high.

Dynamic Programming is basically concerned with decision processes involving a sequence of choices. Many processes that

163

involve continuous decisions through time are of this character. For instance the owner of a fleet of taxis considering when to replace his vehicles could use Dynamic Programming techniques.

These then are the kinds of problems that O.R. has already helped to resolve in industrial situations. Before going on to consider its applicability to educational administration, it is worth re-emphasising two important facets of O.R. Firstly the dependence on models. All the examples given contain models of a kind; in Queueing Theory the model of the queue is an algebraic equation, in Simulation the model is the model! Incidentally, this model itself may contain several models. In Stock Control the model is once again a system of equations which represent the overall cost of storing items which, in turn, has to be minimised by using the mathematical technique of differentiation. In Linear Programming the model is a set of equations which represent the conditions which have to be satisfied. For example each power station must receive enough coal, each pit must have enough coal available, and all transport costs must be minimised. So in this case it is possible to minimise transport costs by manipulating the equations rather than by ordering coal trucks to go from one power station to another and finding out how far they have travelled and how much it has cost.

The second important feature concerns objectives and criteria. These are mentioned earlier in the discussion on defining the problem. The point is that the problem is not resolved unless objectives and criteria have been, in some way, 'optimised'. In Queueing Theory, for example, there are several criteria that might be used. One such would be to minimise the length of the queue, another would be to minimise the waiting time of anybody in the queue, another would be to reduce the risk of anybody finding a queue when he arrived, yet another would be to minimise the overall time taken by the customer to queue and be served. In Stock Control minimisation of overall costs (e.g. tying up capital, placing orders, warehouse space, etc.) is the usual criterion. In the Linear Programming example discussed above the objective was to minimise the overall transport costs. It is easy to see that in industrial situations the relevant objective function is usually explicit and reasonably obvious. In the social sciences, however, such objective functions are less easy to determine and this has been a major barrier in rapidly transferring the treasury of O.R. application from industry to, for example, education and its administration.

The reason why these objectives are difficult to determine is not because they do not exist. It is merely because the objectives used by administrators in the social field, and in education in particular, are difficult to quantify and often difficult to make explicit. However, as every good manager knows, these objectives do exist. Without them, the administrator would not be able to choose between two courses of action and could not take a decision, even to retain the status quo. Intuitively, whether he be concerned with the allocation of children to secondary schools or which teacher should teach a particular class a certain subject, the decision-maker has in the back of his mind a set of criteria which he wishes to satisfy. Moreover, he knows roughly the importance he attaches to each component of the set and if two components conflict, which of the two he would choose. Naturally, many managers would shrink from making these criteria explicit and attaching numerical weights to each of the components. But such difficult hurdles must be overcome for, as decisions get more complex, decision-makers will be able no longer to hide behind vague statements of objectives to prevent the decisions they have taken being questioned.

O.R. and Education Administration

It is convenient, when considering the application of O.R. to educational administration, to classify the field under study. For the sake of exposition, it will be considered that educational administration falls into three categories: national, local and pedagogic. It is recognised that these three categories are by no means mutually exclusive but they form a convenient way for an outsider like an O.R. scientist to study the system at work.

The National Level

At the national level the problems are broad and strategic and the central authority, the Department of Education and Science, rarely has the power to order local authorities to change. Indeed, the most important educational policy change of recent times, the reorganisation of secondary education, is being achieved largely by encouragement and suggestion. How can O.R. help solve strategic problems of this type? It would be presumptuous, in the space of this chapter, to suggest that O.R. can overnight resolve complicated fundamental problems that have taxed some of the best administrators in the country. Moreover, the whole character of O.R. implies a detailed study of all the relevant factors affecting the problem. The discussion that follows, therefore, must be assessed with this in mind. Problems and solutions may be tied together in neat bundles but the only purpose is to illustrate the potentialities of O.R., not to suggest practical outcomes.

A good example of a strategic problem that has already been the subject of much public discussion and been 'solved' at least twice is when to raise the school leaving age to sixteen. It is assumed that the decision to raise the age has been taken and all that is at issue is the timing. This is affected by the size of each school age-group, the supply of teachers, the implementation of new curricula, the provision of buildings, the needs of youth employment and many other things besides. By what criterion should the decision be judged? What are the objectives? The justification for raising the age must rest partially on making a greater contribution to the economic labour force which would imply acting as soon as possible. On the other hand buildings might not be available nor adequate curricula in existence. Because the ultimate decision will affect so many interacting factors a computer model, or simulation, suggests itself. Such a model must be extremely comprehensive to include everything relevant, and yet crude enough to enable the wood to be seen for the trees! In fact a model that might be used for this purpose is being developed by the Unit of Economic and Statistical Studies on Higher Education (Alper, Armitage and Smith, 1967). In this model the educational system is broken down into sectors—Primary Schools, Secondary Schools, F.E. Colleges, Colleges of Education and University. Each sector is broken down into basic elements comprising students and teachers. These elements might be quite specific such as 'Physics

Students, 3rd year' or alternatively quite wide such as 'all mathematics teachers'. The model is concerned with student flows and the likelihood of students moving from one state, say 'fifth form arts', to another, say 'sixth form social studies'. The raising of the school leaving age will affect the chances of changing from one state to another and the model could be run many times to reflect different timings of the decision or strategies such as varying the timing in different parts of the country. Such a procedure would probably reveal a range of years within which it was desirable to raise the leaving age. A network diagram associating the development of curricula and progress of buildings could then be combined with the simulation results to identify the best year or years.

Network Analysis could also be used to study the expansion of the universities, with the nodes of the network representing the size of each university at the relevant time. The interaction on other parts of the educational system and the repercussions on the years ahead can be represented in this way but it may be that at each node an allocation of resources must be made. In this case the problem could be resolved using Dynamic Programming although necessarily such a formulation will involve many simplifying assumptions.

Raising the school leaving age is an example of a rare 'one-off' problem and one that involved direct intervention by Government policy. Many of the problems at the strategic level regularly recur. The allocation of funds for school building between local authorities and between various sectors of education, or the maintenance of the supply of teachers, are examples of problems receiving consideration at frequent intervals.

Problems that involve allocation of scarce resources can often be solved using the Linear Programming methods mentioned earlier. However, this presupposes that objectives can be clearly formulated and quantified and this is no easy task. It might be said that such problems are not suited to O.R. methods and that resources are so scarce that there is little choice. Such a view is not substantiated by the time taken to agree school building programmes nor by the apparent complexity of the exercise with many hundreds of projects going 'into the hat' (Griffith, 1966).

The Local Level

At the local level the education authority can directly execute the results of many of its educational policy decisions. It is constrained by the national policy but within this constraint it has considerable freedom of manoeuvre. This freedom implies choice and thus problems.

There are two reasons why it is easier to recognise the contribution that O.R. can make to local rather than to national educational planning. Firstly, as mentioned above, local education is 'nearer to the ground' and concerned with tactics rather than strategy. Secondly, in the work of the Local Government O R. Unit there are some actual case studies which demonstrate O.R. in action in this field.

The Unit was formally established in April 1965 and is supported by membership of over half the major local authorities in the United Kingdom. It was formed after several years of pioneer work in various aspects of local government service including educational administration. Indeed one of the first major projects involved the development of new methods of forecasting future school populations for a large County Council. The techniques evolved have enabled regular predictions to be made up to ten years ahead for areas containing on average a population of 3000 adults and children. A detailed description of this work can be found elsewhere (Myers, 1966) but it is worth considering the place of forecasting in O.R. Every model of a system should contain some kind of predictive mechanism which estimates how the system will act under certain circumstances. However, the development of this predictive mechanism in itself is not often the most valuable contribution of the model building. The most important aspect is that the whole system should work well or, to return to pupil forecasting, that the figure predicted should be used wisely. The most accurate forecasts in the world are of no avail if subsequent planning is faulty. Thus the most significant contribution that the new schools forecasting work is making is to enable educational planners to react quickly to the otherwise unforeseen and to make more explicit their objectives. This work has now been extended and two additional studies carried out. The first related to the raising of the school leaving age and gave guidance as to the critical factors to measure in the years up to and immediately beyond 1972/73 (Robinson, 1967). The other extension was a special study into the problem of forecasting for new towns (Forsyth, 1967). Several important new models were developed which may well prove of great value in the study of similar problems for other expanding areas.

One problem that appears to lend itself to O.R. methods has arisen out of the reorganisation of secondary education. The implementation of any such plan is often extremely complicated to schedule. For large county areas it is often impossible to make the switch in one step but moving one set of pupils or changing one area obviously has implications on the remainder of the system. What should be done about staff changes? Which buildings should be invested in? The problem obviously needs clear definition but, superficially at least, it appears that network analysis could be used to evolve and assess feasible plans. Once again such assessment implies clarification of objectives and also assessing the cost of falling short of them.

Another problem related to comprehensive reorganisation concerns 'split premises' schools. Many authorities have been forced to aggregate existing physically separate schools into a new single unit. This poses many problems of implementation. What age groups should have which buildings? Should some sections of one building be reserved for certain subjects? Should teachers travel to pupils or vice-versa? To help answer these questions the Unit has developed for four education authorities a computer model of the split-premises school (Nelson, 1968). This model will evaluate in terms of specified criteria the consequences of a given administrative decision. Very often the objective is to minimise pupil travelling and in this case the model would assess the amount of travelling implied by the arrangements above.

From the discussion of Linear Programming it can be seen that there are several areas in local educational administration that might benefit by the application of this technique. The rationalisation of further education in a local education authority or region is one example of this. The problem could crudely be regarded as comprising demands for resources (equipment and/or courses) in different parts of the area in which, however, only limited resources are available in any one place. Moreover there can be different ways of supplying the resources to meet demand in one place as opposed to another each involving different financial and educational costs. This problem could be solved by Linear Programming. Other problems involving the use of limited resources (machines, men and money) can be similarly solved. Specialist equipment, laboratory technicians, investment in special facilities like swimming pools could all be considered as Linear Programmes, provided suitable criteria could be found to evaluate solutions.

As was said earlier it is not really possible to place problems of educational administration in distinct categories such as national, local and pedagogic. In fact there are many problems that cannot be solved without the collaboration of agencies in all three areas. Such a problem is typified by the delays suffered in the school building programme. In the belief that O.R. can make a contribution to this problem the Local Government O.R. Unit, in collaboration with the Department of Education and Science and some education authorities, hopes to undertake a project to establish means to minimise these delays; without joint participation, however, such a study could not be successful.

A further description of the application of O.R. to local educational administration can be found in the Unit's report to the Organisation for Economic Co-operation and Development in August 1966 (Forsyth, et al., 1966). This surveyed the scope for O.R. in this field, reviewed current and past work and presented recommendations as to its future development.

The School

The last category of educational administration, pedagogic, is the most difficult to define. In this context it will be taken to mean the educational system formed by the school, just as the other two categories were defined by systems based on the central and local authorities respectively. In this area the contribution of O.R. may be the most dramatic of all, for the application of O.R. techniques to the actual learning processes will break completely new ground. For the moment some applications of O.R. in the school are reasonably clear to see. Mostly they relate to the utilisation of resources in an efficient manner. This means more than timetabling. Modern educational theory implies more flexibility in the planning of school curriculum, buildings and teachers. To do this teachers must be able to adapt administratively to a changing situation and O.R. can help them to do this. Once again computer models are of obvious value and it is for this reason that the Local Government O.R. Unit have completed an assessment on work in computer methods of school timetabling (Britten and Groom, 1967). The next stage is to assist school building design using computer models like the split-premises model and to develop mathematical methods of programming individual student courses. Austwick's contribution to this book gives a clear statement of some of the problems related to the increasing application of educational technology. Many of the problems— scheduling, optimising the use of resources, investment and replacement—are susceptible to an O.R. approach and it is to be hoped that O.R. will be increasingly used in this field. Similarly Wheeler's contribution outlines many areas in which O.R. can give assistance. The argument for a clear statement of objectives is one that has already been pursued in this chapter.

In this country there has, up to now, been only a limited application of O.R. methods in the school. In the United States, however, several studies have been made using sophisticated techniques.

Abt has formulated the outline of a cost-effectiveness model for an educational system. This overall model in turn breaks down into five sub-models associated with the school, the teaching process, the relationship with the community, and costs and benefits (Abt, 1967). These models have already been applied to studying the reasons why pupils in the U.S. 'drop out' and delineating policy changes to reduce this. In addition the U.S. Office of Education in its survey on the Equality of Educational Opportunity (Stoller, 1967) has carried out some detailed O.R. work at school level that has striking similarities to that of Robinson (1967) at the local authority level in this country. Undoubtedly, the existence of such work indicates the potential that exists for O.R. in this area.

Conclusion

This swift survey indicates the scope and character of the contribution that O.R. is making to educational administration and the potential for increasing this. Moreover earlier experience in Operational Research suggests that close investigation of problems breeds more problems susceptible to its methods. O.R. in education differs from industrial O.R. because of the difficulty in defining objectives, some of which stem from inability to quantify educational and social factors. Such problems are surmountable. What is harder to overcome is the traditional reluctance some administrators have in revealing the basis for their decisions. As the problems facing such men become more complex, it is short-sighted to ignore the help specialists (O.R. men, economists, social scientists, etc.) can provide. It can only be hoped that it will not be necessary to learn by mistakes.

The diversity of the problems amenable to these techniques might bewilder the educational administrator anxious to use this service. When, then, should a problem be tackled by O.R.? First of all it is important to reiterate that O.R. is not a magic wand. Difficult problems can defy satisfactory solution and the best efforts of O.R. specialists. Moreover, if the problem is not complex O.R. may be a sledgehammer to crack a nut. Although sometimes the solution to a problem may look simple, a problem that needs to draw on O.R. very rarely is!

A characteristic of an O.R. problem is that it can be quantified. Sometimes it is difficult for the administrator with a problem to realise this. In such cases the rule is very often 'where there's a will there's a way'. So long as the administrator is willing to see his objectives made explicit in numerical terms—albeit crudely —then the problem will probably be amenable to O.R. techniques. The last prerequisite is that the problem must exist. If only one solution is acceptable there is no choice and therefore no problem. O.R. often vindicates the intuition of the experienced decision-maker but it can only do this when there are a number of possible choices to be made.

In conclusion it should be remembered that like all research O.R. needs an act of faith before it can succeed. To expect solutions to problems before they are studied must mean the problems are not real ones. There are powerful techniques available but every problem is unique and it is only rarely that text-book techniques can be applied without some modification. But with positive encouragement from all concerned with education, O.R. can develop as an important specialist service making a great contribution to the educational system.

Acknowledgement

I wish to thank the Local Government Operational Research Unit and in particular the authors of the reports referred to, for permission to publish details of their work.

References

Abt, C. (1967) *Design for an Education System Cost-Effectiveness Model*, Paris: O.E.C.D.

Alper, P., Armitage, P. and Smith, C. (1967) 'Educational Models, Man-power Planning and Control', London: *Operational Research Quarterly*, XVIII, 2.

Britten, A. and Groom, K. (1967) *The Use of Computers for School Timetabling*, Reading: Local Government Operational Research Unit.

Duckworth, W. (1962) *A Guide to Operational Research*, London: Methuen.

Forsyth, T.H. (1967) *Pupil Forecasting in New Towns*, Reading: Local Government Operational Research Unit.

Forsyth, T.H., Myers, C.L., Robinson, G.M. and Ward, R. (1966) *The Scope for Operational Research in Local Educational Administration*, Reading: Local Government Operational Research Unit.

Griffith, J.A.G. (1966) *Central Departments and Local Authorities*, London: Allen and Unwin.

Myers, C.L. (1966) *New Methods of Forecasting School Populations*, Reading: Local Government Operational Research Unit.

Nelson, M. (1968) *Split Premises Schools*, Report to be published. Reading: Local Government Operational Research Unit.

Rivett, P. and Ackoff, R. (1963) *A Manager's Guide to Operational Research*, New York: Wiley.

Robinson, G.M. (1967) *Staying on at School*, Reading: Local Government Operational Research Unit.

Stoller, D. (1967) *Operations Analysis in the U.S. Office of Education*, Paris: O.E.C.D.

Chapter 10

The Administration of the Larger Educational Unit

G. E. Wheeler

The economies of scale attract the politician, the opportunities of scale fascinate the innovator, the problems of scale intimidate and often overwhelm all but the most competent educationist. To be part of a large system, loosely organised, despite the frustrations of remoteness and insignificance, may be a not unsatisfying experience for the principal of one of the many constituent units, as long as he can fulfil a role acceptable to him as its head. Particularly is this so where a school is small, so that the comfort of intimate association with the group for which he has responsibility is possible. If the unit becomes of such a size that this personal contact is lost, then the administrator has to find new paths to self-confidence in methods of organisation of a hitherto unthought of degree of sophistication.

The movement towards larger educational units is accelerating rapidly and scant attention has been paid in terms of research and hypothesis either to the management of the relatively large educational unit or to the problems of growth or creation that accompany its development. Since most large schools or colleges have grown out of smaller ones, the problems of growth have often been made almost impossible of resolution when the resources, organisational concepts and traditions appropriate to the small scale have been made the resources, concepts and traditions of the large scale.

An attempt will be made in this chapter to look at the management of large scale educational units from experience of technical colleges which have faced, and are facing, the problems of increasing scale and growth. British experience is, of course, a long way behind that of the U.S.A. and the U.S.S.R., but if one believes, as I do, that organisational or management problems are largely sociological and environmental, it is arguable that we should look at our own local experience of change in technical colleges, to see whether that experience can be applied to other educational institutions or analysed in ways that may provide useful insight into our problem.

The technical college, the polytechnic or the college of further education, at any level of size, are undoubtedly most complex educational units; though complexity and scale do not necessarily go together and are not necessarily desirable co-factors in organisation. Present national policy, which aims at the creation of educational units that are both large and comprehensive (e.g. universities, polytechnics, comprehensive schools), may be justified on educational or social grounds. But we know from industrial experience that the objective of rationalisation and simplification must also underlie the success of large scale industrial activity, whether this be measured in terms of profit (presumably a measure unacceptable, however appropriate, to the educationist) or in service to the consumer (an idea which ought, but does not always, coincide with the educationist's actual objectives). Industrial enterprises which aim at complexity and which attempt universality, have had sorry records. If they have achieved a state of quasi-monopoly survival has sometimes been possible by pouring in large resources, but in any situation in which competition for resources has been real, or in which they have been in competition with organisations whose aims have been singular rather than comprehensive, they have been unable to produce an organisation sufficiently effective to survive.

The management of the technical college provides us with a model of great complexity, and it will be useful to identify the factors which create this complexity:

(1) The student body is numerically large—frequently in excess of 10 000.

(2) The attendance of the students is for very varying lengths of time and on a varied organisational basis. Students will be found in large numbers attending:

(i) full-time courses of from one to three years' duration;
(ii) sandwich courses of from three to five years' duration arranged in different time combinations: some students are in the college for alternate periods of full-time study

of six months' duration, others attend for alternate years, and others for varying periods. The sandwich courses may be end-on, in which case one group of students follows another, or they may even overlap;

(iii) block courses, in which students may receive tuition for perhaps one month a year in the college for three years, with intervening attendance of perhaps one day per week;

(iv) part-time day courses: the 'day' lasting from three to twelve hours;

(v) evening courses;

(vi) short full-time courses;

(vii) day conferences;

or, indeed, various combinations of these possibilities.

(3) The college has to be organised so that formal educational processes may take place for twelve to thirteen hours each day for at least five days each week for up to forty-eight weeks each year.

(4) Students, despite the re-allocation of courses deriving from the establishment of the new polytechnic institutes, will be capable in any one institution of working at different rates and intellectual levels, and in a single institution considerable numbers of students will be involved in work in simple crafts and in highly advanced skills. Other students will be undertaking remedial studies, making good deficiencies deriving from the earliest years of their education, whilst still others may be working at post-graduate level.

(5) A 'student' may be anyone from the age of sixteen (or even fourteen where courses are provided in co-operation with a school) through to post-retirement.

(6) Most students will also be engaged in some work activity which will be for them of at least equal significance and may have more importance for them than their college commitments.

(7) The courses provided, the examinations taken, and the actual work, are initiated, assessed or approved by a multitude of examining professional and official bodies.

(8) Because of the variety of age, experience and domicile associated with variations in primary and secondary education,

any 'group' of students is likely to have a very low common factor of capacity in educational skills or experience.

(9) The resources available have rarely been designed for their current education use, and the staff come to technical education with a diversity of experience, training and capacity.

(10) Perhaps most significantly much of the work of these establishments has been initiated quickly on a pragmatic basis to meet an identified need or has been organised to ensure that able students, who would otherwise be deprived of opportunity due to insufficiencies elsewhere in the educational system, should have the opportunity for 'further' education; for example, the current provision for teacher training and the establishment of management training.

(11) A large proportion of the teaching staff are part-time.

The problems faced by colleges can be seen vividly if their situation is likened to that of a factory with 10 000 workers, all of them unskilled in the sense that what they have to do is non-repetitive and new each day, all having to acquire knowledge and skill under the guidance of two or three hundred supervisors who, because the 'workers' are likely to be concerned with most of the skills and knowledge acquired by man, are themselves unlikely to be supervised and helped by highly experienced managers.

Sufficient has been written to illustrate the complexity of activity. Even so the picture given is probably over-simplified, and it may be as well now to consider some of the problems of management of such a unit.

Traditionally colleges have had as their chief executive a principal, who has been answerable to a board of governors, usually a sub-committee of, or answerable to, the education committee of a local education authority. Within the college it has been more common of late for there to be a vice-principal (whose role is often ill-defined), a registrar, and a group of heads of department responsible for major areas of work. The departments have represented broad categories of activity more or less associated with and commonly including Engineering, Science, Commerce, Catering, Building and General Studies. Dependent upon size and local importance departments representing local

177

industries (e.g. mining) or particular specialisms (e.g. mathematics) may appear. Views have differed concerning the optimum size and the optimum range of work to be covered by a department, but generally the opinion has been expressed that there should be 'not too many' departments (about five to six) and that they should be 'not too large' (about twenty to twenty-five staff). Obviously the myths of traditional organisational principle can be sustained where college staff have not exceeded one hundred to one hundred and twenty, but where colleges have grown larger, or where the myths have not been believed, departments with as many as seventy full-time academic staff are to be found, and the range of work within departments may be correspondingly large. Even in a small college a department may embrace an extremely varied group of activities if there are local demands for a wide range of subjects, crafts or skills.

Executive action in colleges has traditionally been centred upon the principal working through a 'heads of department meeting' for general policy development, but at the same time heads of department have had frequently, and of necessity, to organise within the department a structure reflecting the college hierarchy as a whole. Such a hierarchy has probably become unavoidable, given the diversity of work undertaken, and in many colleges the aim has been to achieve growth in order that the work will be sufficient to justify the appointment of appropriate and highly skilled specialist staff. The drawbacks of hierarchies of this kind may be recognised, but practical alternatives when wide-ranging activities have to be undertaken have been slow to appear.

As an objective the educational unit will probably expect to provide the best possible teaching for its students. This can be translated into the policy of having full-time specialists on the staff, but they can be justified only where a sufficient volume of work exists. If the particular needs of the individual or small groups of students are to be met in institutions which are comprehensive, then clearly the institution must be large—probably very large indeed—if it is not possible to provide general as opposed to particular or specialised education.

This kind of hierarchy poses classic problems of communication, integration and evaluation. It even poses problems of the

178

use of the various specialists whose existence may cause the organisation to take the shape it does. In the technical college a variety of means are being experimented with to create feelings of corporateness, to allow for inter-comparison of activity and the establishment of standards. The academic board, representative of the whole college, is perhaps the most significant development, but the creation of subject committees which bring together members of staff of similar disciplines in different departments is also important. Individuals within a department may be given overall responsibility for the teaching of their subject in whatever department it is found. Such a device can obviously create friction and difficulty, in particular where heads still expect all communication to go up and down the line. Courses are frequently and desirably inter-disciplinary, and so it becomes essential for someone to be appointed with overall responsibility for each course. Each course may consist of many groups of students, who must necessarily have tutors well known to them. The tutors must in turn know the students well and be able to answer their queries as to how they fit into the organisation, and ultimately they must be able to tell anyone— principal, head, employer, examiner—something about each student.

The technical college, unlike other educational institutions, has wide external contacts with industry generally, with students' employers, with part-time staff of the college, and with those who have become industrial assessors or examiners. These contacts have to be systematised so that the outside world may readily find access to sources of information and action within the college and so that, conversely, a reasonably coherent approach may be made to the outside world. One way of attempting this is for everything to be channelled rigidly through vertical linear organisational paths, but it can easily be imagined that such communication channels can become clogged and activity and enterprise within the college stultified.

It could be argued that, faced with this situation nationally, locally, and within colleges, organisational laissez-faire is the only practical answer—let everything grow or die where growth or death is natural—be quick to encourage and slow to euthanise. Indeed the random distribution of a wide variety of seeds with

13   179

vigorous application of fertilizer is one fairly sure way of achieving growth, but it does not seem appropriate to the continued management of a large-scale organisation where activities may alter but where the objective may cease to be growth. During the growth period of education, as one of any other activity, buccaneering, opportunism and expediency may be the best that can be hoped for, but these are not the attributes of the larger unit once it has been established, or if they are, society usually finds it desirable or necessary to alter these attributes. It is to the large scale unit that we may consider the application of techniques of organisational analysis.

If we hypothesise that the objective of a student is to reach a given standard in his chosen field of study as easily and quickly as possible, and that the aim of any institution facilitating this activity is to ensure that it is achieved with a minimum of resources, certain organisational and managerial consequences result. It is the failure to recognise these consequences which are the likely causes of difficulty in the administration. The first factor of complexity to be considered is whether attention has been given to the establishment, proclamation and communication of the objectives of the college, and in what way the major and over-riding objectives have been fragmented or lost in establishing individual working environments and tasks for students or teachers. If the argument is accepted that the individual, whether he be student or teacher, must know clearly what it is he is trying to do and what standards of performance—quality, quantity and time-wise—he must reach if he is to have any real chance of integrating his activities with those of his section, department, or college as a whole, then it follows that there must be a very definite commitment to the philosophy of management by objective as enumerated by Drucker (1955), Humble (1965) and others.

In other words for each person in the organisation there must be worked out, with his participation, as complete a statement as possible of his role, his function, his duties and his responsibilities, and this statement should form the basis of his decision-making, his work, and the inevitable assessment of performance which needs to be made to establish how successful or otherwise both he and the organisation are. We find in most colleges that if the simple test is applied of asking students or staff the nature of their organisational (and hence educational) responsibilities, the answers indicate how uncertain people are of what they are about. Indeed, a virtue is often claimed for this uncertainty: syllabuses are withheld from students; one lecturer may be so uncertain of his task that a student has to inform him that work supposed to have been done under another subject heading has yet to be covered; and, worst of all, perhaps neither student nor staff are aware of the inter-relationship of course and subject. In small units such problems of co-ordination can be sorted out by the simple interchange of information on an informal basis. In large educational units internal co-ordination, and the statement of objectives and duties, need to be formalised. Other symptoms deriving from a failure to specify organisational requirements are recognisable in the conflicts and hostilities which arise between departments and disciplines, or the failure to understand the working of the sophisticated control of responsibility systems looked at earlier. The failure to define, delegate and communicate must also lead to many things being left undone which ought to be done, since no complete identification of activity requiring attention and responsibilities to be exercised has been undertaken. The initial preparation of schedules of the type referred to is a large task and presupposes a supply of data and a capacity to plan of a high order. The absence of such capacities and data in a large educational unit can only lead to gross inefficiency, not only in the use of resources from the point of view of the community, but in the output of effort required by the student in directions not central to his study. It is useful to speculate that if success in study requires say 100 units of student effort (however measured), and if the student has the capacity to input say 120 units, if more than 20 effort units are wasted because of organisational weaknesses, deriving from whatever cause, the student will not achieve success. Those who sometimes deplore the apparent unwillingness of students to undertake extra-curricular activities might well ask whether students are, in fact, engaged in using their energies in solving curricular problems which derive from the organisational inefficiencies of the institution. Where the student's potential output is lower how much more vital is it to ensure that each unit is channelled into its most profitable educational use?

Underlying the concept of management by objective is the acceptance of the idea of staff development and recruitment to meet the objectives. Insofar as needs are not clearly defined, staff cannot be selected to fulfil these needs; worse, as time passes needs surely change and some machinery must necessarily exist so that staff may meet the changing educational and organisational demands. The teacher is not a tape recorder into which new tapes can be fed or new programmes inserted. He needs to change not only the content of his teaching but also its method, its approach and his attitude towards it as course and college objectives alter. Essentially the teacher needs to participate in any process of development, and to adjust to changing needs. But in any large educational unit there must be some process of forward planning and current assessment so that there can be assured staff development and change to meet new objectives and responsibilities. Just as with equipment there has to be maintenance, adjustment and occasional scrapping, so if the needs of students are to be met must a programme of re-training and re-adjustment be prepared. For this to be achieved effectively in the large educational unit, a specialist member of staff is probably required to help those of his colleagues whose own capacity or desire for self-development may be insufficient.

The large educational unit needs to apply to its activities the fundamental analytical techniques used in the social services and in industry, such as work study or operational research. In any organisation it is tempting to hope that professionalism and professional standards will ensure proper use of resources and very advanced methods. However, experience shows that when the techniques alluded to are not employed, waste of effort and relative ineffectiveness in the solution of problems are inevitably found. Only by systematic questioning of what is being done and by providing systematic opportunities for creativity can it be reasonably certain that effort and energy are not being wasted, that simpler ways of achieving educational ends are not available. What the student does, what the learning process is, may not lend itself to exploration in this way, but what the teacher does, what the course does, most certainly can be so explored. One result of this kind of concept is programmed teaching, but I would argue that every element of an educational process would benefit from the critical approach of work study. The application of these techniques would be concerned with many aspects of college life—from paper work to justifying the 'even longer' course. One would question the capacity of staff, the methods of teaching, the ability to organise. It might be argued that such questioning would be unprofessional, that the student would suffer, but in hospitals where these techniques have been in use for more than a decade patients have benefited enormously.

The part played by the individual in the educational unit, whether large or small, is significant. We recognise now the necessity of counselling and health services for students. The efficiency of study may be precariously balanced on factors affecting his mental or physical well-being. The teacher, however, is expected to be made of sterner stuff. Whilst college and school authorities have a long history of generosity towards members of staff forced to curtail their careers through illness, the line manager, whether the principal or the head of department, is unsupported by the personnel and welfare staff whose work in industry is so significant. The techniques of selection, training and development are often crude; the absence of staff awareness of developments in the social sciences is an organisational deprivation which can ill be afforded. Again the point is the same; there is within the large educational unit a vast amount of information, education and ability. This is rarely used within the organisation; still less rarely is outside help readily available or sought when essential matters concerning the organisation and its staff are in question. The view has been advanced that in technical institutions the technical education and experience of its chief executives cause them to be suspicious of the social sciences and of anything so imprecise as organisation theory. The more likely truth is that the social sciences and their application have been undervalued in our society, particularly by those in education who might have given a lead in the application of new knowledge and skills.

Organisationally, the large college or school is not the same as a small college or school on a magnified scale. There are different

183

and more opportunities for the employment of specialist staff to meet teaching and organisational needs. It has probably not been sufficiently recognised that the problem of organisation within such units is four-fold:

(1) How may the objectives of the college or school be discovered, developed and defined, and how may an actual organisation be established and managed to meet these objectives?

(2) What kind of effect does the type of organisational framework or machine have on the achievement of any particular objective?

(3) What are the effects of national agreements, directives or policies on the organisation of any particular unit?

(4) What are the expectancies and experiences of those who have the responsibility of determining the organisational structure of colleges or schools?

It is interesting to note under the first of the headings how little research into the working of educational units has been undertaken. Do any colleges have senior staff undertaking research into their own activities and organisation? Any management responsible for the work of 10 000 people, which did not have a management services section undertaking research introspectively, would now be regarded as old fashioned and dangerously so. Following Drucker (1952) we could argue that the problem of determining objectives and standards, or the yardsticks of measurement, is the biggest problem the educational unit has to face. Standards need to be sought for:

(1) The standing of the college.

(2) Innovation: not only innovation in respect of courses, but innovation in respect of skills lying behind the presentation of courses and teaching itself.

(3) The productivity of the institution: by what standards can the achievements of the institution be measured against the resources used: how can increased achievement be attained without using more resources?

(4) What costs are appropriate to various activities; in other words what objective standards can be used to determine the allocation of scarce resources?

(5) The performance of staff, and particularly of 'managerial' staff.

(6) The educational performance of students.

The effect of organisation as an instrument of policy is easily recognised when the process of timetabling is examined. Timetabling, an aspect of the allocation of resources, is now seen as one having complex mathematical determinants. Teaching programmes, student opportunities, staff capacities have to be translated into timetabling strategies. Here there are several problems still to be resolved, but perhaps the most significant is the realisation that many of the limitations thought to be inherent in the timetabling process arise from decisions over policy and from practices which are not themselves absolute. The college or school which complains of shortage of a particular form of accommodation may be creating the 'shortage' by deciding to use it only between certain hours. The utilisation of accommodation in particular can be much increased by altering the parameters within which decisions are commonly made. Indeed the acceptance of particular 'forms' of course may impose utilisation difficulties which disappear when other course profiles are adopted. More significant would be a wider understanding of forms of organisation by college staff, by the recognition that certain organisation structures are likely to bring prophesiable advantages or difficulties and the recognition that college staff need to be trained to recognise the significance of different organisational strategies. This could lead to the exploitation of advantages and the avoidance of pitfalls. All organisation is an aspect of specialisation, but a failure to recognise the significance of the categories and types of relationship established leads, particularly in large units, educational or otherwise, to lower levels of achievement than would otherwise be the case. Most of us have been brought up in relatively simply organised institutions. We have notions of organisational lineality and leadership, which are incapable of efficient expression in large scale units. The frequently recognised problems of delegation and acceptance of responsibility stem from naive concepts of administrative approaches. Highly sophisticated human relationships and expectations must be developed and catered for in a large educational unit where it is impossible to build on the thesis of a strong central motivation.

All colleges and schools are necessarily affected by and are in turn able to affect other institutions. Obviously the larger the unit the greater the forces at work are likely to be. It may be hypothesised that many large units have paid insufficient attention to the society or community in which they exist. The image, the role, the reputation of the institution will affect the resources it can command. The college needs to recognise the industrial concept of marketing at two levels. Its customers, its students, will themselves be influenced by the reputation of the college they attend. If they feel that it is third or fourth best, insufficiently understood and insufficiently supported by industry or society, they themselves will lose self-confidence. A small institution hardly expects to be widely noticed. The expectation of prestige in a large institution is great and if not achieved the disappointment stemming from unfulfilled expectations is likely to affect the work of the institution. What applies to students applies equally to staff. The provision of resources will also largely depend upon how fully the institution is accepted by its environment and how well it understands its role. If a college of technology, for example, through its action or inaction leads industry to feel that it has a contempt for industrial opinion, it can hardly expect significant industrial support in terms of the sponsorship of students and the provision of research and other funds. Certainly the absence of an 'authoritative' voice for technical education has harmed its reputation.

Educational institutions have traditionally strong underlying despotic tendencies. The opportunities for intellectual and personal exploitation have too often been taken, so that in looking at the expectancies and experiences of those who have responsibility for organising the structure of a large educational institution the following will have to be considered:

(1) How far a despotic system of organisation is felt to be appropriate either by those within or responsible for particular institutions.

(2) If it is the common experience, how may attitudes be altered if different forms of relationship are required.

186

(3) How effective the large unit can be if it is to be genuinely based on a non-despotic situation and if there is little real experience amongst the staff or students of a college of non-despotic organisational possibilities.

The practical problems may be illustrated by a simple case. The principal of a college reflecting the spirit of an academic board may give departmental heads wide freedom for the development of work and methods for which they have responsibility. A department head may in turn establish an area of work for which a principal lecturer has responsibility, hoping that within that area similar freedom will be established for more junior staff. The principal lecturer, however, is autocratically efficient and does not see his objective as including the development of freedom and responsibility for the staff for whose work he has responsibility. In due course the junior staff move on, but their experience of organisation is uncreative and is likely to be reflected in their own subsequent management. Because of the scale of operation in the larger educational unit the identification of situations such as these is difficult and can probably be overcome only by the concept of management by objective outlined earlier.

Conclusions

The organisational process is an experimental one. In small educational units the types of experiment possible are few. The needs are simple and thus effective results can usually be achieved whatever accident or chance decrees. The competence and enthusiasm of good teachers more than compensates for all but the worst administrative travesties. The problem of the larger educational unit is that the experiments possible are of such a scale and substance that the range of effectiveness is magnified. The organisation can dominate the individual or student. It can frustrate him, lessen his capacity to work, and pose problems which despite his goodwill are beyond his ability to resolve. That this can and does occur in the larger educational unit is not to condemn its size. It is rather to suggest that the management of the unit must be more than proportionately capable of growth and development. Just as poor management in larger educational units is more frustrating than poor management in small units, effective management in large units can add dimensions of experience, opportunities and variety of stimulation, which are entirely beyond the resources of smaller units, and this is the organisational justification of the larger unit. However, there must be recognition that in large units the process of organisation requires at least as much study and attention as the process of education. If benefits derivable from large scale units are to be enjoyed, the formulation of the organisational design, the role of the individual educationists and administrators who are its executives, and the demands made upon teachers and students, need extremely careful analysis and integration.

Technical colleges as well as other educational institutions have shown remarkable growth capacities. The excitement and challenge of growth have often provided stimulus to staff and students sufficient to overcome obvious organisational deficiencies. What is important is to recognise that when growth ceases, inertia should not replace stimulus; that inefficiency or frustration should not be regarded as the inevitable price paid for being large. It is worth quoting from Edwards and Townsend (1959):

There is no point at which an organisation must become *less* efficient than it would be if it were smaller; but beyond the point where economies...of large organisation are exhausted, it will not be *more* efficient.

Bibliography

Argyris, Chris (1960) *Understanding Organisational Behaviour*, London: Tavistock Publications.

Brown, W. (1960) *Exploration in Management*, London: Heinemann.

Drucker, Peter F. (1955) *The Practice of Management*, London: Heinemann.

Edwards, R.H. and Townsend, H. (1959) *Business Enterprise*, London: Macmillan.

Humble, J.W. (1965) *Improving Management Performance*, London: British Institute of Management.

Likert, R. (1961) *New Patterns of Management*, New York, London: McGraw-Hill.

McGregor, D. (1960) *The Human Side of Enterprise*, New York, London: McGraw-Hill.

Miller, E S. and Rice, A.K. (1967) *Systems of Organisation*, London: Tavistock Publications.

Index